D1713467

REMOTE SENSING for LANDSCAPE ECOLOGY

New Metric Indicators for
Monitoring, Modeling, and
Assessment of Ecosystems

REMOTE SENSING for LANDSCAPE ECOLOGY

New Metric Indicators for
Monitoring, Modeling, and
Assessment of Ecosystems

Robert C. Frohn

Department of Geography
University of Cincinnati
Cincinnati, Ohio

LEWIS PUBLISHERS

Boca Raton Boston London New York Washington, D.C.

Acquiring Editor:	Jane Kinney
Project Editor:	Andrea Demby
Marketing Manager:	Arline Massey
Cover Design:	Dawn Boyd
PrePress:	Carlos Esser
Manufacturing:	Carol Royal

Library of Congress Cataloging-in-Publication Data

Frohn, Robert C.
  Remote sensing for landscape ecology : new metric indicators for monitoring, modeling, and assessment of ecosystems / Robert C. Frohn.
       p.   cm.
    Includes bibliographical references (p.   ) and index.
    ISBN 1-56670-275-5 (alk. paper)
    1. Landscape ecology—Remote sensing. 2. Geographic information systems. I. Title.
QH541.15.L35F76 1997
577'.028—dc21
                                                                            97-31769
                                                                                 CIP

© 1998 by CRC Press LLC
Lewis Publishers is an imprint of CRC Press LLC

No claim to original U.S. Government works
International Standard Book Number 1-56670-275-5
Library of Congress Card Number 97-31769
Printed in the United States of America 1 2 3 4 5 6 7 8 9 0
Printed on acid-free paper

Preface

The broad goal of this book was to develop improved metrics that show predictable or independent responses to characteristic variation in remote sensing data, specifically spatial resolution, while showing most-sensitive responses to actual changes in landscape pattern. To achieve this goal two objectives were accomplished. The first objective was to develop landscape metrics that were sensitive to changes in fragmentation and patch shape complexity along various predictable gradients of change. The second objective was to develop landscape metrics that were insensitive or predictable with changes in spatial resolution.

The improved metrics developed were the *Patch-Per-Unit* area (*PPU*) metric and the *Square Pixel* (*SqP*) metric. *PPU* measures the degree of fragmentation of patches on a landscape, and *SqP* measures the shape complexity of patches on a landscape. These two metrics were analyzed and compared with two traditional metrics for fragmentation and patch shape complexity: *Contagion* and *Fractal Dimension*. The metrics were applied to four study sites that exhibited one of three predictable gradients of change: a spatial horizontal gradient; a vertical gradient; and a temporal gradient.

For the spatial gradient, two test sites were used. The first site was located in central Rondônia, Brazil, where deforestation decreases as a function of distance from a major urban center. The second site was a large metropolitan area of Washington, D.C. and adjacent areas of natural vegetation and crops. For the vertical gradient, the study site chosen was a vertical transect in the Sierra Nevada range, California, from alpine areas to Bakersfield, California. The final temporal study site was located in the Ouro Prêto colonization area of the Amazon Basin of Rondônia, where Landsat images and a clearing simulation model of the area were utilized.

For all four study sites, both *PPU* and *SqP* performed as predicted exhibiting the ability to distinguish among landcover types and landscape changes, unlike *Contagion* and *Fractal Dimension*. For the Rondônia study site, both *PPU* and *SqP* performed as predicted exhibiting the ability to distinguish the amount of deforestation as a function of distance from an urban center. For the Washington, D.C. area study site the *PPU* and *SqP* metrics were able to distinguish among nine landcover categories, including evergreen needle leaf forest; deciduous broadleaf forest; mixed forest; grasslands; shrub lands; wetlands; croplands; urban; and water. For the Sierra Nevada study site both *PPU* and *SqP* were able to distinguish among seven landcover categories, including urban; chaparral; forest; alpine; large agricultural fields; small agricultural fields; and medium-sized agricultural fields. Finally, for the Ouro Prêto study site, *PPU* and *SqP* exhibited expected temporal patterns.

The *PPU* and *SqP* metrics were also found to be predictable with spatial resolution. The *PPU* metric exhibited a negative log/log correlation with spatial resolution. Regression analysis of *PPU* for the log transformations yielded R^2 values above 0.95 for all four study sites. *SqP* showed a near linear trend for all four study sites. Linear regression analysis of *SqP* also had a high R^2 (>0.95) value for all four study sites indicating a strong linear correlation between *SqP* and spatial resolution. The traditional metrics of *Contagion* and *Fractal Dimension* showed no predictive capability for all four study sites and exhibited counterintuitive results in most of these sites.

This book has demonstrated the need for increased research on the integration of remote sensing, geographic information systems, and landscape ecology metrics for modeling, monitoring, and assessment of ecosystems. The long-term value of such research will be realized as we employ these technologies and methods to achieve an improved understanding of the world in which we live.

Because this book is concerned with improvement of landscape ecology metrics, it may appear critical of other studies that have used or developed traditional metrics. It is not the author's intention to suggest that all or any of these other studies are invalid. The author apologizes to any of the authors cited who have been given the impression that their work has been perceived as invalid. Quite the contrary, without these studies the groundwork would not have been made for the quantitative improvement in the field of landscape ecology. The author is indebted to the researchers of these studies, especially those that have been devoted to the development of traditional landscape ecology metrics.

About the Author

 **Robert C. Frohn, Ph.D.,** is a research professor of Geography at the University of Cincinnati, Ohio. He received his Ph.D. from the University of California, Santa Barbara, his Masters from Miami University, Ohio, and his B.A. from Thomas More College.

Dr. Frohn's research areas include satellite remote sensing, geographic information systems, landscape ecology, tropical ecology, and quantitative methods. His research has been funded by the National Aeronautics and Space Administration (NASA), the Environmental Protection Agency (EPA), the Department of Energy (DOE), and the California Space Institute, among others.

Dr. Frohn is the founder and director of the Environmental Monitoring and Remote Sensing program (EMARS) at the University of Cincinnati. He is a member of numerous organizations and committees, including the American Society for Photogrammetry and Remote Sensing (ASPRS), the Association of American Geographers (AAG), the Urban and Regional Information Systems Association (URISA), and the International Association of Landscape Ecology (IALE).

Acknowledgments

The author is very grateful to the many fine people who have contributed to this book. I am especially thankful to Jack Estes for providing guidance, support, and advice for the past seven years, as well as for providing comments to this manuscript. I am also especially grateful to Ken McGwire who provided inspiration, guidance, technical support, and canned-heated discussions during the course of this effort. I thank many people who have provided or offered comments and criticisms to this manuscript, including Virginia Dale, Mike Goodchild, Dar Roberts, and several anonymous reviewers. I also thank the many graduate students who have provided technical or moral support throughout this research work in the Remote Sensing Research Unit, University of California, Santa Barbara (UCSB). I especially thank Bill Starmer for help with graphics and the Washington, D.C. study site. I thank Gunter Menz, University of Bonn, Germany for help with the Sierra Nevada study site. For programming support, I thank Ken McGwire, Kurt Riitters, and Sidey Timmins. I also thank Bob O'Neill for discussions in the past involving landscape metrics. For logistical support I thank the Geography Research Office at UCSB, 3rd Floor Ellison, including Beilei, Kathleen, Nancy, Tacy, Tracy, and Theresa. I also thank Joel Michaelsen of UCSB and Boyoung Lee and Robert South of the University of Cincinnati. Finally, I thank all my family, friends, and colleagues who have supported me throughout the course of this research effort. I hope you know who you are. This research was funded in part by grants from the National Aeronautics and Space Administration, the Environmental Protection Agency, and the California Space Institute.

Dedication

This book is dedicated to the sweet memory of my two best friends, Elbert Christie and Norbert Frohn.

Contents

CHAPTER 1

Introduction

This book introduces two improved metrics of fragmentation and patch shape complexity for landscape ecology analysis of remote sensing images. Quantitative measurements of landscape pattern have been used in the field of landscape ecology for nearly a decade (Krummel et al., 1987; O'Neill et al., 1988). These measurements, often called metrics or indicators, have been used to link ecological and environmental processes with patterns found on the landscape. The three most commonly used metrics have been *Dominance*, *Contagion*, and *Fractal Dimension*. These metrics will be discussed in more detail below and in Chapter 2.

Various landscape ecology metrics have been used to quantify aspects of spatial pattern and correlate them to ecological processes (O'Neill et al., 1988; Turner and Gardner, 1991; Baker and Cai, 1992; McGarigal and Marks, 1994; Riitters et al., 1995). In particular, spatial pattern metrics of *Contagion* and *Dominance* (based on information theory) and *Fractal Dimension* (based on fractal geometry) have been used extensively throughout the landscape ecology community (e.g., Krummel et al., 1987; O'Neill et al., 1988; Turner and Gardner, 1991; Milne, 1991; Wickham and Riitters, 1995). These three metrics have also been proposed for implementation as watershed integrity indicators, landscape stability and resilience indicators, and biotic integrity and diversity indicators by people who have worked on the U.S. Environmental Protection Agency (EPA) Environmental Monitoring and Assessment Program (EMAP) (EPA, 1994). Unfortunately, to date there have been few tests of these metrics by the remote sensing community (e.g., Wickham and Riitters, 1995; Wickham et al., 1996; O'Neill et al., 1996). An extensive review and analysis of the literature concerning these metrics suggests a number of conceptual problems with metric development and implementation.

The *Dominance* metric has been used as a landscape diversity measure by determining the equality of the proportion of landcover types on the landscape (O'Neill et al., 1988). High *Dominance* indicates that one or more landcover types are covering the landscape. Low *Dominance* indicates that landcover types have nearly equal proportions. However, *Dominance* does not necessarily indicate diversity of the landscape. For example, a landscape with two landcover types with 50% proportion will have the same *Dominance* value as one with ten landcover types with 10% proportion. Thus, the same arguments that apply to species diversity indexes apply to the *Dominance* landscape metric of diversity. Also, the *Dominance* metric does not actually give a quantitative measurement of landscape pattern, although it has been referred to as a spatial metric. For these reasons, the *Dominance* metric was not analyzed in this book, but rather mentioned only because of its association with the two other metrics: *Contagion* and *Fractal Dimension*.

The *Contagion* metric has been used in ecosystem analysis to quantify the amount of clumping or fragmentation of patches on a landscape (O'Neill et al., 1988). It has been utilized to relate the effects of *Contagion* patterns on ecosystem processes such as habitat fragmentation, vegetation dispersal, and animal movements (Turner and Ruscher, 1988; Turner, 1989, 1990a, 1990b; Graham et al., 1991; Gustafson and Parker, 1992; Li and Reynolds, 1993; EPA, 1994; 1996). The *Fractal Dimension* metric has been used in ecosystem analysis to quantify the complexity of patch shapes on a landscape (Krummel et al., 1987; O'Neill et al., 1988; De Cola, 1989; Lam, 1990). It has been used as a measure of the degree of human disturbance on the landscape. The premise is that natural boundaries such as those for vegetation have more complex shapes than those that are a result of human activity, such as agricultural fields. As human disturbance increases, the *Fractal Dimension* of the landscape decreases (Krummel et al., 1987; O'Neill et al., 1988; Turner and Ruscher, 1988; De Cola, 1989). Despite their widespread use, the *Contagion* and *Fractal Dimension* metrics have not been thoroughly evaluated as to their sensitivity to variations in remote sensing data and raster data structures. Furthermore, these metrics were originally developed to focus attention toward quantification of landscape pattern and to encourage the development and application of new or improved metrics in ecosystem analysis (O'Neill, 1996, personal communication).

The utility of a landscape metric is dependent on its maintaining a consistent response to observed phenomena. This does not occur when the fundamental assumptions applied in its formulation are violated. Even in cases where the use of a *Contagion* or *Fractal Dimension* metric may be appropriate, there are a number of characteristics that affect the quality of map and image data including spatial resolution, geometric registration, and level of classification. The ability of *Contagion* and *Fractal Dimension* to maintain a consistency of response across varying spatial resolutions does not appear to have been thoroughly considered in the implementation of *Contagion* and *Fractal Dimension* in landscape ecology research. It is a central contention of this research that these characteristics may have significant effects on the estimated *Contagion* and *Fractal Dimension* for landscape representations derived from digital maps and remote sensing data. In order for a landscape metric to be effective it should be relatively insensitive to arbitrary sampling characteristics while being very sensitive to the specific spatial patterns. Since remote sensing and other landscape data are captured in a wide variety of geometric representations, landscape metrics must be formulated to compensate for specific sampling geometries in order to facilitate comparison and integration across scales and among different studies.

1.1 GOALS AND OBJECTIVES

The goal of this research was to develop improved metrics that are independent of characteristic variation in remote sensing data, specifically, spatial resolution, and most sensitive to actual changes in landscape pattern. In order to achieve this goal two major objectives were met. The first objective was to develop metrics that were sensitive to changes in fragmentation and patch shape complexity along various predictable gradients of change. The second objective was to develop metrics that behaved predictively with changes in spatial resolution while being most sensitive to various predictable gradients of change. The second objective is very critical because if landscape metrics are unpredictable with changes in spatial resolution, then changes in metric values may be a function of spatial resolution in addition to changes in landscape pattern. Thus, one would not know whether the change in the metric values was due to actual landscape pattern changes or due to characteristic variation of remote sensing data.

The goals and objectives of this book were met by carrying out a series of tasks. These tasks include

1. A review of landscape ecology metrics currently being used for the monitoring and assessment of landscape change and the understanding of ecosystems.
2. An evaluation of the landscape metrics of *Contagion* and *Fractal Dimension* on a conceptual basis using a systematic approach to the design of the metrics.
3. The development of improved metrics to resolve problems identified with *Contagion* and *Fractal Dimension* as landscape metrics.
4. A comparison of *Contagion* and *Fractal Dimension* empirically with improved metrics using "real-world" data for various gradients of change.

1.2 SIGNIFICANCE OF RESEARCH

Landscape metrics are employed to create quantitative measures of spatial patterns found on a map or remote sensing image. One can look at a map or image and notice a number of patterns. Perhaps the landscape is full of rectangular geometric shapes, indicative of agricultural fields. Or, one might find an image that contains an array of adjacent circles, indicative of fields with center point irrigation systems. In other areas we may see a regular grid of intersecting lines, such as those often found in residential areas. One may notice in a scene that there are many elongated complex shapes such as those found in association with geologic formations. Or there may be a series of thin elongated narrow strips with a more regular shape, indicative of folded mountain ridges and valleys. One may notice the fish bone pattern of deforestation in Rondônia, or large rectangular fields of deforestation in central Amazonia.

We may also notice the arrangement of patches across a landscape. Perhaps they are fragmented into thousands of small patches such as in the Chesapeake Bay area. Or, they may consist of large patches of forest and large clear-cuts such as those in the Upper Northwest of the U.S. Basically, when one views a satellite image he or she may notice or identify many elements which when combined characterize the physical aspects of the scene. These elements include tone or color, shadow, illumination, location, association, objects, and process. In addition, the person may notice varying shapes, size of shapes, textures, and patterns. It is the quantification of these groups of elements into a measurable variable that the use of landscape metrics allows. Thus, all of the patterns mentioned above can be quantified and distinguished from one another through the use of landscape metrics. But why is it so important to quantify these patterns if we can see them? One reason is that not all images can be described by an observer. Consider the complex geomorphic, geologic, soil, and mountain formations in New England surrounding the Adirondacks. How does one describe the shapes, patterns, and textures of this area in a few words? Landscape metrics can potentially quantify these spatial patterns in one or two variables. But, more importantly, the use of landscape metrics by researchers can facilitate the detection of patterns of change that are not readily visible to the human eye nor easily detectable by a human analyst.

The most important reason landscape metrics are necessary is so that landscape patterns and ecological and environmental processes can be linked quantitatively. Landscape ecology is the study of the effects of landscape patterns and their changes on ecological processes. By quantifying spatial patterns and their changes we hope to quantify their effect on ecological processes. Thus, we can study changes in habitat of a particular species or community of organisms and determine whether or not the habitat has become too fragmented for the species or community to survive or remain stable. We can determine the complexity of shapes of a given habitat type and determine if certain animals will migrate or interact given the number of edges between various landcover types, all from the use of landscape metrics with remote sensing data.

There are a number of areas in geography, particularly remote sensing and geographic information systems (GIS), where this book can make a significant contribution. One fundamental contribution is that this book will help continue bridging a long-standing gap between landscape ecology and geography. More specifically, this book will help to bring knowledge concerning quantitative landscape ecology to users of remote sensing and GIS. Remote sensing has long been used as a means for providing data for environmental studies. However, to date the use of remote sensing to characterize landscape patterns and relate them to ecological processes has not been thoroughly addressed.

On the other hand, this book may have just as large an impact on landscape ecology studies. This is due, in part, to the fact that the field of geography is much larger than that of landscape ecology, but more so, in part, because an increase in exposure to remote sensing and geographic information knowledge might help increase the application of this geographic knowledge to other studies in the field of landscape ecology.

There are a number of other contributions that this book can make to geography, particularly remote sensing and GIS. First, the improved and tested metrics could be used to improve classification of remote sensing data. For instance, some of the work accomplished in the conduct of this research allowed for the ability to distinguish different categories of landcover based on the metric values alone. In plotting a new fragmentation index against a shape complexity index, there was better distinction between landcover categories using the landscape metrics than using any spectral plots. This discovery gives notion to what I refer to as a "spatial signature" of a given landcover type. By putting more emphasis on spatial pattern with landscape metrics for landcover classification or combining landscape metrics with spectral information, classification of remote sensing data can be greatly improved. This is a topic for further investigation.

This book strongly emphasizes the importance of a data structure in the analysis of landscape pattern. This book emphasizes the importance of spatial resolution for detecting spatial patterns and changes on the landscape. This emphasis is of great importance because of the use of remote sensing to monitor global landcover change. I maintain that validating thematic global landcover proportions is simply not enough in evaluating and performing cross-sensor comparisons and that the consideration of global land-use patterns must be addressed (Frohn and Estes, 1996). I hope others will agree, because research derived from this book can help provide a sensible and simple means for performing such analyses.

Some of this research involved going back to the classical analysis of spatial pattern literature 40 to 50 years ago (e.g., see Hagget et al., 1977). The development and use of basic principles of scale in geography and geographic data structures, and application of them to the development of metrics that are independent of characteristic variation, such as spatial resolution, should be a significant advance that can be applied to other research in the fields of geography, remote sensing, and landscape ecology.

1.3 SELECTION OF STUDY SITES

Various study sites were chosen for this research. Study sites were chosen in areas where gradients of change in spatial pattern could be identified and analyzed. It was decided to use spatial (spatial horizontal), vertical, and temporal gradients to get a diversified selection of study sites.

For the spatial horizontal study site two Landsat Thematic Mapper (TM) scenes were analyzed. The first was a Landsat TM image in central Rondônia for June, 1986 (path 231, row 67) where the landcover consists of forest and cleared agricultural areas of farmer settlements. The second study site was an area of an October 1989 Landsat TM scene located northwest of Washington, D.C. with Frederick, Maryland in the north, Leesburg, Virginia in the southwest, and Gaithersburg, Maryland in the southeast. In this area, nine distinct classes were identified. They consist of (1) evergreen needle leaf forest; (2) deciduous broadleaf forest; (3) mixed forest; (4) shrub lands; (5) grasslands; (6) wetlands; (7) croplands; (8) urban; and (9) water.

The study area chosen for analysis of changes along a vertical gradient was an August, 1990 Landsat TM scene of the high mountain ecosystem of the Sierra Nevada range, California. The transect in this study is located along an extreme vertical gradient from the summit areas of Sierra Nevada to the bottom of the central valley between Fresno and Bakersfield, California. The area encompasses a wide spectrum of vertical vegetation zones. Changes in landcover are predominately correlated with changes in altitude, as reflected in maps of California's natural vegetation and potential vegetation. A classification scheme was used consisting of the following landcover types: (1) alpine; (2) forest; (3) chaparral; (4) small agricultural fields; (5) medium-sized agricultural fields; (6) large agricultural fields; and (7) urban areas.

The site chosen for a temporal gradient of change was the colonization area of Ouro Prêto, located in the south-central Amazon Basin of Rondônia, Brazil. In Ouro Prêto, clearing of tropical forests for agriculture has occurred since 1972 due to road building and the settling of farmers on individual 100-ha lots (Frohn et al., 1990). Such a process results in fragmentation of undisturbed tropical forest into thousands of patches of forest and cleared areas. Patterns found in this study area represent over two decades of human forest clearing for agriculture and cattle raising. A data set was developed covering an area of 254,000 ha consisting of archive maps of lot boundaries for the area, Landsat Multispectral Scanner (MSS) scenes (path 248, row 67) for 1973, 1978, 1980 and Landsat TM scenes (path 231, rows 67, 68) for 1986. In addition, work with researchers at the Environmental Sciences Division, Oak Ridge National Laboratory has resulted in the development of a model which simulates spatial patterns in this area (Southworth et al., 1991; Dale et al., 1993a). The model has been validated with the Landsat data and determined to simulate land-use change patterns similar to those occurring in Ouro Prêto (Frohn et al., 1996). The model allowed for analysis of the sensitivity of the landscape metrics over a longer period of time than could be accounted for by the Landsat data alone.

1.4 SUMMARY OF CHAPTERS

This book is divided into five chapters. In addition to the Introduction, Chapter 2 is a background chapter which describes and evaluates in more detail the principles behind landscape ecology metrics. Sections 2.1 through 2.3 describe potential problems that may exist when using traditional landscape ecology metrics with remote sensing or raster data. Section 2.4 introduces the improved metrics and how they alleviate problems that have been identified with the traditional metrics. The final section evaluates the traditional and improved metrics systematically using simulated and test images.

Chapter 3 gives a detailed description of the methodology used in addressing the goal of this book. Section 3.1 presents an overview of the experimental design used to approach the two major objectives of the book. Sections 3.2 and 3.3 give a detailed description of the overall methodology followed throughout the course of this research. A number of subsections follow to point out modifications to the methodology for various study sites.

Chapter 4 presents the results and discussion for the various study sites. Chapter 4 is divided into 4 subsections each focusing on the type of landcover change: spatial, vertical, and temporal. For each subsection two issues are addressed: (1) the sensitivity of the traditional and improved metrics to actual changes in landscape pattern, and (2) the sensitivity of the traditional and improved metrics to spatial resolution.

The final chapter gives a summary and conclusions derived from this study. It also gives recommendations as to the proper use of the improved metrics in landscape ecological analysis. Finally, Chapter 5 presents a number of other uses that landscape metrics may potentially provide for applications in remote sensing and geographic information research.

CHAPTER 2

Background and Evaluation of Landscape Metrics

Landscape ecology has been broadly defined as the study of the effect of landscape pattern on ecological processes (Turner, 1989). With this definition, one can clearly see that in order for such a discipline to continue advancing, methods are needed to quantify landscape pattern so that measurable links to ecological processes can be determined. The most common method for quantifying landscape patterns is to capture information of a particular spatial pattern into a single variable. Such variables are commonly referred to as landscape metrics or landscape indexes.

There are a number of terms and concepts related to landscape metrics and remote sensing that need to be defined before discussing landscape ecology metrics.

The sampling unit used in remote sensing and raster data is referred to as a picture element or pixel. Generally, a pixel is a square, having four sides or edges. A pixel can also be an equilateral triangle, a hexagon, or any other equilateral tessellation.

A contiguous cluster (using the cardinal rule) of homogeneous pixels is referred to as a patch. For example, a patch can be a lake, a tract of forest, or any group of pixels that is homogeneous with respect to a certain classification. A mosaic of patches across a given area constitutes a landscape.

There are a number of terms that describe patterns found on a landscape. These terms include diversity, dominance, contagion, fragmentation, and patch shape complexity. Each of these terms has a variety of definitions in landscape ecology, geography, and remote sensing. For the purposes of this book, we will use a single working definition for each term. First of all, we define diversity of a landscape as the total number of landcover types. This definition is often referred to as landscape richness (Forman and Godron, 1986; Forman, 1995). Second, dominance is defined as the degree to which one or a few landcover types predominate the landscape in terms of proportion (Forman and Godron, 1986).

The next two terms, contagion and fragmentation, are opposites of one another. Contagion is the tendency of landcovers to cluster or clump into a few large patches (Wickham et al., 1996). On the other hand, fragmentation is the tendency of landcovers to break up into many small patches (Forman, 1995). A landscape with high contagion would be one with low fragmentation, and a landscape with high fragmentation would be one with low contagion. Thus, even though contagion is not defined as a measure of fragmentation, it is directly related to fragmentation. Also, it is important to know that both terms, contagion and fragmentation, are relative to both spatial resolution and ecological process. For example, a 30-m landscape with a particular configuration might be considered fragmented. Whereas a landscape at 1 km spatial resolution with the same configuration may be considered to have a high contagion and low fragmentation. In the same respect, a landscape may be considered to have high contagion and low fragmentation for a large predatory bird, while the same landscape may be considered fragmented and have low contagion for a small avian flycatcher.

The final term, patch shape complexity, refers to the relationship between the perimeter of a patch and the area of the patch. In general, complex patches are those that have greater scaled perimeter-to-area ratios, while simple patches are those that have lower scaled perimeter-to-area ratios. Once again, this term is relative to both spatial resolution and ecological process.

Just as these terms have a variety of definitions, they are quantified in a variety of ways. This quantification is termed a landscape metric. In this book traditional metrics for measuring contagion and patch shape complexity are compared with two new metrics. The traditional metric for contagion is referred to as *Contagion* and for patch shape complexity as *Fractal Dimension*. To avoid confusion with defined terms, all metrics will be italicized, while the conceptual terms defined above will not be italicized. *Contagion* will be contrasted to an improved metric called *Patch-Per-Unit area* (*PPU*), and *Fractal Dimension* will be contrasted to an improved metric called the *Square-Pixel* (*SqP*) metric.

2.1 LANDSCAPE ECOLOGY METRICS

There is a wide variety of landscape metrics and many software programs to calculate them (O'Neill et al., 1988; Turner and Gardner, 1991; Baker and Cai, 1992; McGarigal and Marks, 1994; Riitters et al., 1995). Many of these metrics have been shown to be highly correlated with one another (Riitters et al., 1995). In a factor analysis study, Riitters et al. (1995) analyzed 55 landscape metrics for their statistical independence. They concluded that the information contained in the 55 metrics could be narrowed down to 6 metrics. These include

1. *Dominance*;
2. *Contagion*;
3. *Fractal Dimension from Perimeter/Area*;
4. *Average Patch Perimeter/Area Ratio*;
5. *Average Patch Perimeter/Area Ratio Orthogonally Adjusted*; and
6. *Number of Classes*.

The EPA ranked the status of a number of landscape metrics into one of three categories: for use as watershed integrity indicators (Table 2.1); landscape stability

Table 2.1 Ranking of Watershed Integrity Indicators by the EPA (EPA 1994)

	Status
Contagion	C
Fractal Dimension	C
Dominance	C
Lacunarity	A
Erosion risk	A
Flood indicator	A
Riparian zones	C
Loss of wetlands	C
Agriculture near water	B
Miles of new roads	B
Amounts of agriculture and urban	C
Watershed/water quality indicator	A

Note: A = requiring further conceptual development; B = requiring testing for feasibility/sensitivity; C = ready for field tests and implementation.

Source: Environmental Protection Agency, Landscape Monitoring and Assessment Research Plan, EPA 620/R-94/009, Office of Research and Development, Washington, D.C., 1994.

Table 2.2 Ranking of Landscape Stability and Resilience Indicators by the EPA

	Status
Contagion	C
Fractal Dimension	C
Dominance	C
Lacunarity	A
Diffusion rates	A
Percolation backbone	B
Percolation thresholds	B
Miles of roads	B
Recovery time	A
Landcover transition matrix	A

Note: A = requiring further conceptual development; B = requiring testing for feasibility/sensitivity; C = ready for field tests and implementation.

Source: Environmental Protection Agency, Landscape Monitoring and Assessment Research Plan, EPA 620/R-94/009, Office of Research and Development, Washington, D.C., 1994.

and resilience indicators (Table 2.2): and biotic integrity and diversity indicators (Table 2.3). The three rankings employed by the EPA relate to the metrics readiness for use by personnel in their work (EPA 1994). The rankings are

(A) Requiring further conceptual development;
(B) Requiring further testing for feasibility/sensitivity; and
(C) Ready for field tests and implementation.

In all cases, *Contagion* and *Fractal Dimension* were given the highest ranking, C, indicating that they were ready for field tests and implementation.

Furthermore, the EPA (1994, p. 26) maintained that change in landscape patterns could be characterized by the three metrics of *Contagion, Fractal Dimension*, and

Table 2.3 Ranking of Biotic Integrity and Diversity Indicators by the EPA 1994

	Status
Contagion	C
Fractal Dimension	C
Dominance	C
Lacunarity	A
Change of habit	C
Habitat for endangered species	C
Loss of rare landcover	C
Corridors between patches	B
Amount of edges	C
Edge amount per patch size	B
Patch size distribution	C
Largest patch	B
Interpatch distances	B
Linear configurations	A
Actual vs. potential vegetation	B
Wildlife potential	A
Miles of new roads	B
Diffusion rates	A
Percolation backbone	B
Percolation thresholds	B
Resource utilization scale	B
Scales of pattern	A
Cellular automata	A
Pixel transitions	A

Note: A = requiring further conceptual development; B = requiring testing for feasibility/ sensitivity; C = ready for field test and implementation.

Source: Environmental Protection Agency, Landscape Monitoring and Assessment Research Plan, EPA 620/R-94/009, Office of Research and Development, Washington, D.C., 1994.

Dominance (Figure 2.1). Change in the landscape would then be analyzed by calculation of three-dimensional Euclidean distance as

$$\text{Change} = \left((X1 - X2)^2 + (Y1 - Y2)^2 + (Z1 - Z2)^2 \right)^{1/2} \tag{2.1}$$

where, in this example, X is *Dominance*, Y is *Contagion*, and Z is *Fractal Dimension* and at some magnitude (as yet unknown) this shift would represent a phase change in the landscape (EPA, 1994).

2.2 THE *CONTAGION* METRIC

The *Contagion* metric was first proposed by O'Neill et al. (1988) and later by several others (Turner and Ruscher, 1988; Turner, 1989, 1990a, 1990b; Graham et al., 1991; Gustafson and Parker, 1992; Li and Reynolds, 1993; EPA, 1994; 1996) as a measure of clumping or aggregation of patches. It is also used as an indication of the degree of fragmentation of a landscape. *Contagion* is given as

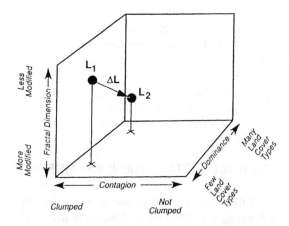

Figure 2.1 Three-dimensional conception of landscape characterization according to the EPA (1994). *Fractal Dimension* is a measure of patch shape complexity. *Contagion* is a measure of clumping or fragmentation. *Dominance* is a measure of the evenness of landcover proportions.

$$Contagion = \frac{2\ln(t) + \sum_{i=1}^{t}\sum_{j=1}^{t}\left(\left(n_{ij}/N\right)\ln\left(n_{ij}/N\right)\right)}{2\ln(t)} \tag{2.2}$$

where n_{ij} is the number of shared pixel edges between classes i and j and N is twice the number of total pixel edges since there is double counting of edges (e.g., AB and BA edge counted twice) and t is the total number of classes. Twice the natural log of t reaches its maximum when all pixel edges of classes i and j have the same proportion. In such a case, a given pixel of one landcover type would have an equal chance of being adjacent to another pixel of any landcover type. Division by twice the natural log of t normalizes the value of C between 0.0 and 1.0. Theoretically, at lower values of C, there are many small patches, and thus the proportion of pixels being adjacent to a given landcover type are nearly equal. As *Contagion* approaches 1, there are large contiguous patches on the landscape (O'Neill et al., 1988; Li and Reynolds, 1993).

The *Contagion* metric has been used extensively in the analysis of landscapes and ecosystems. *Contagion* has been used to detect changes in spatial patterns of clumping across a variety of landscapes in the U.S. (O'Neill et al., 1988; Turner and Ruscher, 1988; Turner 1990a, 1990b; EPA, 1994; 1996; Riitters et al., 1995) and the Brazilian Amazon (Dale et al., 1993b; 1994). *Contagion* has been used to detect the effects of spatial scale on landscape patterns (Turner, 1989). *Contagion* has also been used to analyze the relationship between landcover proportions and spatial pattern (Gustafson and Parker, 1992). Graham et al. (1991) used *Contagion* in ecological risk assessment. And, Musick and Grover (1991) used *Contagion* as a measure of image texture. These are just a few examples of the use of the *Contagion* metric.

Despite its widespread use, *Contagion* may be adversely influenced by a number of problems that have not been thoroughly addressed with respect to remote sensing data. The following is a list of potential problems with the *Contagion* metric that are addressed in this book:

1. Effects of measurement resolution on *Contagion*;
2. Effects of raster orientation on *Contagion*; and
3. Effects of varying the number of landcover classes on *Contagion*.

2.3 THE FRACTAL DIMENSION METRIC

Fractal Dimension has been used for measurement, simulation, and as a spatial analytic tool in the mapping sciences. *Fractal Dimension* has also been used to characterize landscape complexity (Krummel et al., 1987; O'Neill et al., 1988; De Cola, 1989; Lam, 1990). The term "fractal" was introduced by Mandelbrot (1977) and its range of applications later developed and expanded to other disciplines (Lam and Quattrochi, 1992). An overview of fractals can be found in Goodchild and Mark (1987).

The use of fractals in remote sensing is relatively new (Lam and Quattrochi, 1992). Several studies have used fractal analysis with remote sensing images (De Cola, 1989; Lam, 1990; Agnon and Stiassnie, 1991; Linnet et al., 1991; Meltzer and Hastings, 1992). Lam (1990) found that different landcover types had different *Fractal Dimensions* for each band of a Landsat TM scene. Lam (1990) also maintained that the use of fractals on individual bands may serve as guidelines in the future for selecting bands for display and analysis.

Changes in Fractal Dimensions in remote sensing images have implications for changes in environmental conditions (Lam and Quattrochi, 1992). A number of studies have found that the *Fractal Dimension* of the landscape varies according to the type of land use (O'Neill et al., 1988; De Cola, 1989). For example, forest areas tend to have more complex shapes and manifest high Fractal Dimensions while agricultural areas tend to have simple shapes and thus have low Fractal Dimensions. There also appears to be a correlation between *Fractal Dimension* and the degree of human disturbance of the landscape (Krummel et al., 1987; O'Neill et al., 1988; Turner and Ruscher, 1988; De Cola, 1989). As human disturbance increases (e.g., increased intensity of cultivation), the *Fractal Dimension* of the landscape decreases (Krummel et al., 1987; O'Neill et al., 1988).

There are a number of methods that can be used to determine Fractal Dimension of a landscape (Lam and Quattrochi, 1992). The most common method of determining Fractal Dimension on images in landscape ecology is based on perimeter-to-area relations. Fractal dimension as originally derived by Mandelbrot (1977) describes a scale invariant power relationship between perimeter and area in the form:

$$P = kA^{D/2} \tag{2.3}$$

where P = perimeter
       A = area

D = Fractal Dimension

k = constant of proportionality

Fractal dimension, D, may then be determined from Equation 2.3 as

$$\ln P = \ln\left(kA^{D/2}\right) \tag{2.4}$$

$$\ln P = \ln k + \ln\left(A^{D/2}\right) \tag{2.5}$$

$$\ln P = \ln k + (D/2)*(\ln A) \tag{2.6}$$

$$D = 2*\left(\ln(P) - \ln(k)\right)/\ln(A) \tag{2.7}$$

The value of D is between 1 (with simplest shapes) and 2 (most complex shapes) (O'Neill et al., 1988).

Landscape ecologists have been using this perimeter-to-area relationship with map and image data to characterize the complexity of landscape patterns (Krummel et al., 1987; O'Neill et al., 1988). The *Fractal Dimension* of landscapes has been most commonly estimated by regression methods (Krummel et al., 1987; O'Neill et al., 1988; Milne, 1991; Baker and Cai, 1992; McGarigal and Marks, 1994). Referring to Equation 2.6, the natural logarithm of perimeter is regressed against the natural logarithm of area for all patches on the landscape. The $\ln(k)$ is the y-intercept and for squares $k = 4$. *Fractal Dimension* is estimated as two times the slope of the regression since the slope is $D/2$.

Although the result has been referred to as Fractal Dimension, this is an inappropriate use of terminology both in conceptual foundation and technical implementation. The presupposition in this use of Fractal Dimension is that self-similar patterns exist across various sizes of landscape patches, which are in turn much larger than the measurement resolution. Fractal Dimension is a measurement across scales which is predicated on the concept of actual or statistical self-similarity across measurement scales. Determining a dimension from perimeter/area relationships for patches of a landscape at a single measurement scale is not Fractal Dimension. In other words, patches of different sizes at one scale are used as a surrogate for a change in scale.

Furthermore, unless the constant of proportionality (k) is known, there are two unknowns in Equation 2.7. Regression takes care of the unknown $\ln(k)$ by determining the y-intercept. The constant of proportionality (k) is only known for geometric equilateral shapes (e.g., a square) and true fractals (e.g., a Koch curve). The value of k is the constant that relates the perimeter of a shape to the square root of the area of a shape. For instance, for a square $P = 4 * A^{1/2}$; thus, $k = 4$. For other geometric equilateral shapes $P = k * A^{1/2}$ and for fractal shapes $P = kA^{D/2}$ (Equation 2.3). The question remains whether or not the $\ln(k)$ (i.e., y-intercept) is estimated correctly for other shapes during regression in estimating *Fractal Dimension*. This question is raised in more detail in Section 2.6.

The trend toward the use of *Fractal Dimension* as a general index of landscape pattern or complexity is evidenced by the number of studies that have utilized it as a metric. The majority of studies for the use of *Fractal Dimension* using linear regression in landscape ecology concerns changes in landcover patterns from broad scales (Gardner et al., 1987; Lathrop and Peterson, 1992; Riitters et al., 1995) to regional scales (Iverson, 1988; Turner and Ruscher, 1988) to local scales (Pastor and Broschart, 1990; Rex and Malanson, 1990; Mladenoff et al., 1993). Sugihara and May (1990) showed a number of applications of *Fractal Dimension* in ecology. Gustafson and Parker (1992) used *Fractal Dimension* to examine the relationship of landcover proportion to landscape pattern. Dale et al. (1993b; 1994) used *Fractal Dimension* to characterize simulated spatial patterns in the Brazilian Amazon. The importance of *Fractal Dimension* is further shown by the recent EPA recommendations that it is a technique which is ready for field tests and implementation in its Environmental Monitoring and Assessment Program (EMAP) (EPA, 1994; 1996).

The *Fractal Dimension* metric has embedded in it a fundamental assumption that there is a power law relationship between perimeter and area. This assumption may often be violated in dealing with both landscape and remote sensing data. Despite its widespread use, the fundamental concepts in the formulation of *Fractal Dimension* and the perimeter area regression technique for determining *Fractal Dimension* have not been thoroughly addressed. Furthermore, the sensitivity of *Fractal Dimension* to variations in the sampling geometry of remote sensing data and raster data structures also needs to be examined. The following is a list of potential problems with *Fractal Dimension* as a landscape metric of shape complexity that are addressed in this book:

1. Problems with perimeter/area regression;
2. Problems of *Fractal Dimension* with the raster data structure; and
3. Effects of measurement resolution on fractal dimension.

2.4 INTRODUCTION OF IMPROVED METRICS

Based on potential problems with *Contagion* and *Fractal Dimension*, which are discussed in detail in Sections 2.5 and 2.6, improved metrics were developed for quantifying landscape pattern that are less sensitive to spatial resolution and problematic geometric characteristics of the raster data structure. The metrics are introduced in this section and will be used in comparison to *Contagion* and *Fractal Dimension* throughout this book. For quantifying landscape clumping, *Contagion* is contrasted with an alternative metric called *PPU*:

$$PPU = m/(n * \lambda) \qquad (2.8)$$

where m is the total number of patches, n is the total number of pixels in the study area, and λ (is a scaling constant equal to the area of a pixel (note that this area could be expressed in any convenient units, i.e., m^2 or ha). In this book, *PPU* is always expressed in km^2 unless otherwise noted. *PPU* is low when the landscape is not fragmented. As the landscape becomes more fragmented, *PPU* increases. Because it is scaled to actual area, *PPU* is predictable with changes in measurement

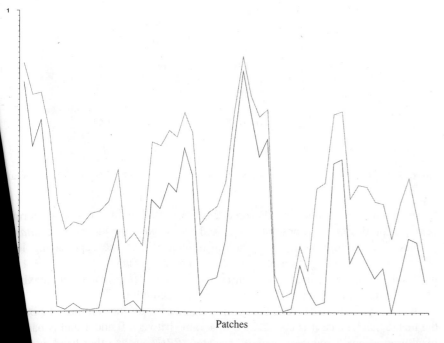

Patches

2.3 Graph showing correlation between *Dominance* (top) and *Contagion* (bottom) for patches on a sequoia landscape.

umber of Classes, Contagion, and PPU

agion is not only a measure of aggregation but also a measure of diversity. *n*, like the *Dominance* metric, is based on the Shannon evenness measure a measure of species diversity or patch diversity (O'Neill et al., 1988; al., 1995). The correlation between *Dominance* and *Contagion* can be there are few landcovers, such as aggregations of patches on a sequoia n Figure 2.3.

 dditional classes are added, the *Contagion* value increases. Figure 2.4 andscapes that are exactly the same in terms of clumping or fragmen-iffer only in number of classes. The value of *Contagion* changes from The value for *PPU* on the other hand, remains the same (13.8). In this *tagion* is obviously more sensitive to diversity than pattern. In a study nd Riitters (1995), data were aggregated from 4 to 80 m and *Contagion* en though an analysis of covariance indicated significant differences gated *Contagion* values, the authors maintained that the statistical nificant because the slopes of the covariance estimates were too flat. t the slopes were flat is because the authors were using 23 classes; was measuring diversity more than clumping.

diversity factor and therefore is unaffected by changes in the number measures only pattern (i.e., fragmentation or clumping). The value

---

resolution unlike *Contagion*. As the landscape becomes more generalized and contagious due to resampling, *PPU* decreases in the expected manner. Thus, it was hypothesized that *PPU* would give a better and more predictable quantification of landscape clumping or fragmentation than *Contagion* because it is less sensitive to spatial resolution and more sensitive to landscape pattern.

As an alternative to *Fractal Dimension* for quantifying patch shape complexity, *SqP* is introduced. The *SqP* considers the perimeter area relationship for raster data structures and normalizes the ratio of perimeter and area to a value between 0 (for squares) and 1 (maximum perimeter, edge, deviation from that of a perfect square). *SqP* is given as

$$SqP = 1 - \left(4 * A^{1/2}/P\right) \qquad (2.9)$$

where A is the total area of all pixels and P is the total perimeter of all pixels in the study area.

SqP is unitless and predictable with measurement resolution. *SqP* also provides an important alternative to *Fractal Dimension* because it does not assume a power law relationship between perimeter and area and, thus, provides a more-effective metric for landscapes which do not exhibit statistical fractal geometry. If the user does not wish to constrain the values of *SqP* between 0 and 1, a simple transformation of $1 / (1 - SqP)$ gives a scaled perimeter-to-area ratio that ranges from 0 to infinity expressed as *Sq*, which equals: $P / 4 * A^{1/2}$. The nonconstrained form of *SqP* (*Sq*) may be more desirable for examining spatial separability of landcover types, for instance, to improve spectral classification of remote sensing data. This gives rise to a notion that I refer to as a "spatial signature" (Frohn, 1996).

2.5 POTENTIAL PROBLEMS OF TRADITIONAL LANDSCAPE METRICS FOR USE WITH REMOTE SENSING DATA

As presented in the lists at the end of Sections 2.2 and 2.3, there are a number of potential problems associated with the application of *Contagion* and *Fractal Dimension* with remote sensing or other raster data. This book primarily focuses on problems associated with spatial resolution and introduces two metrics that alleviate those problems. Spatial resolution is exclusively dealt with because remote sensing data come from a variety of sensors that differ in spatial resolution. In addition, map and other GIS raster data once acquired can be represented at an unending number of spatial resolutions. What is required are metrics that are insensitive or predictable with changes in measurement resolution. Without such metrics, integrated investigations of landscape patterns that employ multiple sensor data products may prove to be invalid. In addition, problems associated with the number of classes and raster orientation on *Contagion* are indirectly addressed empirically in this study because the improved metric alleviates such problems. The problems with both metrics, *Contagion* and *Fractal Dimension*, will be evaluated systematically with the improved metrics in the next section using test figures and simulated images.

In general, the following reasons account for the problems encountered with *Contagion* and *Fractal Dimension* in landscape analysis. These problems will be addressed more specifically below. It was the identification of these problems that facilitated the development of the improved metrics.

Fractal Dimension does not consider the basic perimeter/area relationship of a raster data structure, it has inherent problems with its regression estimation, and does not give consistent results for landscapes with predictable geometric shapes. The *Contagion* metric is based on pixel adjacency proportions, and thus is very dependent on spatial resolution. The *Contagion* equation itself measures not only clumping but also diversity and thus can give biased estimates depending on the diversity of the landscape. The development of the improved metrics has taken a number of factors into account, such as eliminating the diversity factor in the *Contagion* equation and considering the perimeter-to-area relationship of raster data structures for a complexity index that is improved over that of *Fractal Dimension*.

2.6 SYSTEMATIC EVALUATION OF LANDSCAPE METRICS

In this section I demonstrate with simple test images and figures the specific problems with *Contagion* and *Fractal Dimension* and how they are alleviated with the improved metrics of *PPU* and *SqP*, respectively. Again, the problems that are given the most attention are those that deal with spatial resolution. Potential problems with number of classes and raster orientation for *Contagion* are also touched upon here to caution the reader that they may exist.

2.6.1 Problems with *Contagion*

The problems with spatial resolution, class number, and rotation with remote sensing and other raster images are due mainly to two elements of the *Contagion* equation. First, the *Contagion* equation is based on pixel adjacency proportions, and, second, the equation not only measures clumping or fragmentation, but also diversity of landcovers.

Please, refer to the *Contagion* equation (Equation 2.2) for easy reference. Recall n_{ij} is the number of shared pixel edges between classes i and j, N is twice the number of total pixel edges (since there is double counting of edges, e.g., AB and BA edge counted twice), and t is the total number of classes. Twice the natural log of t reaches its maximum when all pixel edges of classes i and j have the same proportion.

(1) *Spatial Resolution,* Contagion, *and* PPU

The double summation terms of the *Contagion* equation are based on the proportion of pixels that are adjacent to one another. They are also summed and give a negative value. Thus, when pixel adjacency proportions are equal, the double summation variable of the equation reaches its absolute value maximum, $2 \ln(t)$, and *Contagion* is zero, meaning minimum clumping or maximum fragmentation.

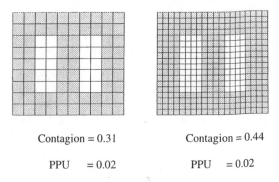

Contagion = 0.31   Contagion = 0.44

PPU   = 0.02   PPU   = 0.02

Figure 2.2 The effects of pixel size changes on *Contagion* and *PPU* for id patterns.

As pixel adjacency proportions become less equal, the double sum the equation decreases in absolute value and thus *Contagion* incre reaches its maximum when one landcover dominates the landsca proportion of pixel edges adjacent to the same class. Therefor $\ln(1) = 0$. Thus, we have $2 \ln(t) / 2 \ln(t) = 1$ and *Contagion* rea of 1 with maximum clumping and minimum fragmentation.

As a result, the *Contagion* equation is dependent on the the image. And, since it is constrained to a value between 0 a pixel proportions, *Contagion* cannot be scaled. *PPU*, on the based on the total number of patches (m) and the total num image. Thus, a scaling constant can easily be applied by size of the pixels.

The influence of pixel size on *Contagion* is shown in Fi represent the same landscape, but halving the cell incre to 0.44. The value of *PPU* remains the same, 0.02, w fragmentation. The scaling constant used incorporate between the two images are not the same.

The rates of change in *Contagion* values are rel of patches on the landscape. Edge pixels will decre patch pixels. Edge pixels decrease at a linear rate patch pixels decrease at an exponential rate. Thus, value of *Contagion* will depend on the proportio (100% proportion adjacent to the same landcover adjacent to the same landcover). The rate of de square patch can be determined from the scale

For within-patch pixels the rate is (A_{scale} * patch pixels the rate is $A(A_{scale} - 1)$, where A to go from 3 m to an aggregation of 9 m reqi window is used. The rate of decline of withi pixels, while the rate of decline for betwe The reverse is true for replicating pixels. T to between-patch pixels becomes greater

Figure 2.4   The effects of varying the number of landcovers on *Contagion* and *PPU*. *Contagion* increases from 0.25 to 0.41 with the increase in number of landcovers, while *PPU* remains the same (13.8).

of *PPU* would be affected only if aggregation or some other manipulation changed the actual pattern of the landcover types. For example, if aggregation resulted in five classes from an original ten classes, then *PPU* would most likely change, as it should, because the pattern would most likely change.

(3) *Raster Orientation,* Contagion, *and* PPU

Raster orientation affects the value of *Contagion* by changing the pixel adjacency proportions. The more rectilinear an image, the more within-patch pixels and the greater the value of *Contagion*. Figure 2.5 demonstrates this hypothesis. The figure is a series of rectangles that are rectilinear in orientation. The value of *Contagion* changes from 0.21 to 0.03 as the image is rotated 45° to the North. The reason for the change is that the rectangles in the original image have more within-patch pixels than the rotated image, and thus *Contagion* is higher. The rotated image below has more edge pixels and fewer within-patch pixels, and *Contagion* decreases.

The values for *PPU* remain the same for the two images (164.5). The reason *PPU* remains constant is that the number of patches and number of pixels remains constant. Since *PPU* is only dependent on these two factors in the two images, the value is unchanged. It should also be noted that the value of *PPU* is rather high indicating a fragmented landscape, which it is for the scaling factor used. The scaling factor used was 0.009 to simulate a TM image. Other scaling factors would change the overall value of *PPU* but not between the two images. For example, using a scaling factor of 1 simulates National Oceanic and Atmospheric Administration Advanced Very High Resolution Radiometer (NOAA AVHRR) data and results in a value of 0.148 for both images. At such a resolution, *PPU* recognizes that the landscape is not very fragmented, which is intuitive since the image would be much coarser with the same number of patches.

Figure 2.5   The effects of rotating a simulated landscape 45° on the values of *Contagion* and *PPU*. *Contagion* decreases from 0.21 to 0.03, while *PPU* remains constant (164.5).

(3) Does the Contagion *Metric Measure Contagion?*

Due to the various problems presented with the *Contagion* metric, a critical question arises: Does the *Contagion* metric actually measure contagion? Recall that in Chapter 2 contagion was defined as the tendency of landcovers to cluster or clump into a few large patches. Since it has been demonstrated that *Contagion* is dependent on the number of pixels, spatial resolution, number of classes (i.e., diversity), and raster orientation, the answer to the question is, not always.

The *Contagion* metric has been interpreted in the literature as various measurements of the landscape. O'Neill et al. (1988) called the metric a measure of contagion. Li and Reynolds (1993) referred to the *Contagion* metric as a landscape complexity measure. Wickham and Riitters (1995) interpreted *Contagion* as a measure of edge-type evenness. A similar variation of the *Contagion* metric was interpreted as a measure of image texture by Haralick et al. (1973). In a recent paper by Wickham et al. (1996) analyzing the *Contagion* metric it was concluded that the metric was a measure of contagion (i.e., the tendency of a landcover to cluster into a few large patches).

To conclude this section, it is demonstrated that even in cases where *Contagion* is not affected by the number of pixels, spatial resolution, number of classes, or

A	A	A	B	B
A	A	A	B	B
A	A	A	B	B
C	C	C	C	C
C	C	C	C	C

Contagion = 0.22

PPU   = 0.12

A	A	A	B	C
A	A	A	C	B
A	A	A	B	C
B	C	B	C	B
C	B	C	B	C

Contagion = 0.42

PPU =   0.68

Figure 2.6 A case where the *Contagion* metric does not measure contagion. The figure at the top is a 5 × 5 image of three classes which appear contagiously distributed. The figure at the bottom appears fragmented with 17 patches for the three classes. However, the *Contagion* metric is lower (0.22) than the fragmented image (0.42). *PPU*, on the other hand, recognizes that the top image (0.12) is much less fragmented than the bottom image (0.68).

raster orientation, there can be many instances where the *Contagion* metric does not measure contagion. An example is presented in Figure 2.6. The image on the top contains three landcovers that are clumped into three patches. The image on the bottom contains the same three landcovers that are fragmented into 17 patches. According to the *Contagion* metric the image at the top should have a higher value than that on the bottom since the top image is contagiously distributed while the bottom image is more fragmented. However, the value for *Contagion* on the top image is 0.22 and the value for the bottom image is 0.42. Clearly, in this case the *Contagion* metric does not measure contagion. There are many other cases in which *Contagion* gives counterintuitive results.

PPU, on the other hand, recognizes that the image on the top is less fragmented and more clumped than the image on the bottom. The values for *PPU* using pixel units as a scaling factor are 0.12 for the top image and 0.68 for the bottom image. This example demonstrates the contrasting conceptual approaches to measuring landscape clumping or fragmentation. The *Contagion* metric is based solely on pixel adjacency and number of classes without considering the patch as a measuring unit. *PPU*, on the other hand, considers both the number of patches and the number of pixels and can be scaled to reflect the spatial resolution of the image.

2.6.2   Problems with *Fractal Dimension*

This section evaluates the stability of *Fractal Dimension* in characterizing shape complexity for remote sensing or raster data. Specifically, most problems with the use of the *Fractal Dimension* metric to evaluate landscape pattern quantitatively lie in two areas. The first is that *Fractal Dimension* assumes a power law relationship with some sort of statistical self-similarity for patches on the landscape. The second, and probably most important, is that the use of perimeter area regression creates a multitude of problems including goodness of fit, spread of data, calculation of the true *y*-intercept, and need for an adequate number of patches. None of these problems is encountered when using *SqP*.

(1)   Regression Estimates and Fractal Dimension

The most popular method of estimating *Fractal Dimension* in landscape ecology is by means of linear regression (Krummel et al., 1987; O'Neill et al., 1988; Milne, 1991; Baker and Cai, 1992; McGarigal and Marks, 1994). To estimate *Fractal Dimension (D)* by regression, (Equation 2.6), $\ln(P)$ is plotted against $\ln(A)$ for all patches and *D* is estimated as two times the slope of the fitted line with $\ln(k)$ being the *y*-intercept. The regression technique was introduced in the landscape ecology literature by Krummel et al. (1987) and O'Neill et al. (1988). Lovejoy (1982) first used this method to estimate the *Fractal Dimension* of clouds. Clearly, as in any other type of regression analysis, a visual inspection of the regression fit is required. Linear regression is based on a number of assumptions, and this may be further compounded by the assumption that perimeter and area maintain a power law relationship. Regression estimates of *Fractal Dimension* are sensitive to the number of patches that is used in the estimation, the range of patch sizes, and the mixing of landcover types with different perimeter/area relationships with a single-scale estimate of *Fractal Dimension*.

Typically, in assessing the fit of a regression estimate one might use a statistical parameter such as R^2. However, a high R^2 value does not always indicate a reasonable estimate of *Fractal Dimension*. For example, the regression estimation method for the landscape in Figure 2.7a which simulates forest clearing in the Amazon provides a *Fractal Dimension* estimate of 0.40 with an R^2 of 0.79. Though the R^2 is relatively high, according to the *Fractal Dimension* equation the estimate of 0.40 is impossible (a value of 1 is the theoretical minimum according to the equation). Now consider Figure 2.7b which is the modeled deforestation for the same area 1 year later. One would expect that Figure 2.7a and b would have relatively similar values since the landscapes appear similar in terms of patch complexity. The perimeter/area regression method for Figure 2.7b yields a *Fractal Dimension* of 1.2 with an R^2 of 0.81.

The problem in this example of regression estimates is the small number of patches and a very limited range of perimeter/area values among the patches. In Figure 2.7a all of the patches have similar perimeter/area ratios so there is little leverage on which to base a regression estimate. In Figure 2.7b a slight change in the perimeter/area values among patches allows for an apparently reasonable calculation.

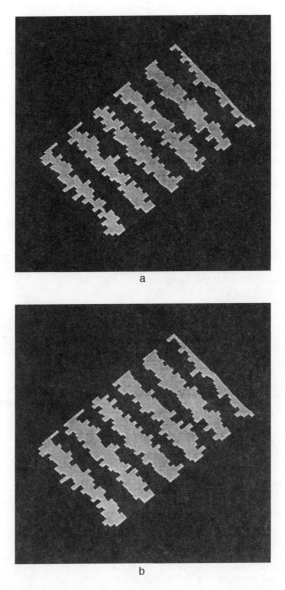

Figure 2.7 (a) A simulated image in a 300-km² colonization area of central Rondônia for 1978. The *Fractal Dimension* for this image was 0.40 which according to the *Fractal Dimension* equation is impossible. The value for *SqP* is 0.9186. (b) A simulated image in a 300-km² colonization area of central Rondônia, Brazil for 1979. The *Fractal Dimension* for this image was 1.20 which according to the *Fractal Dimension* equation is reasonable. The value for *SqP* is 0.9179.

SqP does not have the problems that *Fractal Dimension* has for calculating perimeter-to-area relationships. *SqP* for Figure 2.7a is 0.9186 and 0.9179 for Figure 2.7b.

Although the perimeter/area regression method is referred to as *Fractal Dimension*, it actually is not. Fractal Dimension is a measurement across scales. With the

		P	A	LNA	LNP
Perimeter:	20				
Area:	25	1X	20	25	3.2188758	2.9957323
Resolution:	1	2X	40	100	4.6051702	3.6888795
		3X	60	225	5.4161004	4.0943446
		4X	80	400	5.9914645	4.3820266
				0	1.386
					Y-intercept
			SLOPE	0.5	1.3862944
				1	
			R-SQUARE	1	

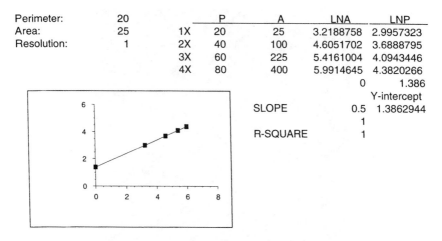

Figure 2.8 *Fractal Dimension* of a square using perimeter/area regression across scales. The slopes of the regression is 0.5 which gives a *Fractal Dimension* of 2 ∗ 0.5 = 1 as it should. Note that the *y*-intercept is 1.3862944.

		P	A	LNA	LNP
Perimeter:	22.8				
Area:	25	1X	22.8	25	3.2188758	3.1267605
Resolution:	1	2X	45.6	100	4.6051702	3.8199077
		3X	68.4	225	5.4161004	4.2253728
		4X	91.2	400	5.9914645	4.5130549
				0	1.517
					Y-intercept
			SLOPE	0.5	1.5173226
			Fractal Dim	1	
			R-SQUARE	1	

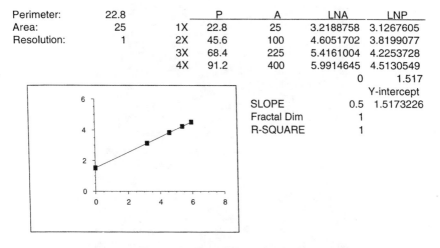

Figure 2.9 *Fractal Dimension* of a triangle using perimeter/area regression across scales. The slopes of the regression is 0.5 which gives a *Fractal Dimension* of 2 ∗ 0.5 = 1 as it should. Note that the *y*-intercept is 1.5173226.

perimeter/area regression method *Fractal Dimension* is estimated at a single scale with the assumption that the power law relationship and statistical self-similarity will exist for different size patches across the landscape. The *Fractal Dimension* metric was given its name because a log vs. log plot of patches over the scales of patches on the map can be self-similar and that this self-similarity is demonstrated by the significance of the regression, i.e., R^2. Clearly, R^2 is not a proper diagnostic for statistical self-similarity as shown above. In fact, there is no diagnostic which can test for statistical self-similarity using these methods.

A significant problem in calculating *Fractal Dimension* using the perimeter/area method is the value of the y-intercept. If the Fractal Dimension was calculated properly, such as by scaling the data and plotting $\ln(P)$ and $\ln(A)$ for each scale and then taking two times the slope, one will get different y-intercept values depending upon the shape(s) that is scaled. This is because the y-intercept is equal to the $\ln(k)$. For example, Figure 2.8 shows a regression plot of Fractal Dimension for a square. The slope is 0.5; thus, Fractal Dimension is 1.0 which is what it should be and the R^2 value is 1. Note the y-intercept in this case is $\ln(4) = 1.386$. Figure 2.9 shows the same plot for triangles. Again, the slope is 0.5 giving a Fractal Dimension of 1.0 and an R^2 of 1. However, the y-intercept has changed to $\ln(((0.5 \sin(60))^{1/2} / 3) = \ln(4.56) = 1.517$.

The constant of proportionality (k) is determined by the relationship between perimeter and area for a particular shape. For hexagons, the y-intercept is $\ln(3.72) = 1.314$, and, for circles, the y-intercept is $\ln(3.54) = 1.264$. So then, what happens if one mixes triangles, squares, hexagons, and circles at one scale on the landscape. Theoretically, the Fractal Dimension should be 1.0 since all are equilateral shapes. Figure 2.10 shows the result of mixing triangles, squares, hexagons, and circles at one scale on the same landscape. The value of *Fractal Dimension* was 1.34 which is an incorrect value for the four geometric shapes which according to the Fractal Dimension equation equal 1. The new y-intercept was 1.168 which is lower than any of the four geometric shapes. However, the R^2 was high at 0.996 indicating a good fit. Such a process is what occurs when one measures Fractal Dimension at one scale for many different shapes. There is a mixing of patch shapes which may be self-similar or even fractal, but, because these shapes have different values for k, the Fractal Dimension is estimated incorrectly. The process is even worse for patch shapes that have unknown k values and thus unknown Fractal Dimensions. The estimate of k then becomes a mixed value of different-shaped patches where the perimeter-to-area constant of proportionality may differ significantly as shown in Figure 2.10.

Figure 2.11 shows the correct method of scaling to estimate Fractal Dimension applied to a Sierpinski carpet which is a true fractal. The Fractal Dimension was 1.89 which is correct for a Sierpinski carpet with an R^2 value of 1, a k value of 1, and a y-intercept of $\ln(1) = 0.0$. The process would become even more complicated and incorrect if the *Fractal Dimension* of a landscape consisting of multiple shapes were measured at one scale (e.g., a set of Sierpinski carpets, squares, and triangles). However, this process is exactly what occurs when one mixes different-shaped patches at a single scale for estimating Fractal Dimension using perimeter-to-area regression. Thus, estimating Fractal Dimension by regression at a single scale for different patches with different origins and slopes creates a value which is incorrect and uninterpretable.

If there were enough samples, such as an infinite number, then the fit of the slope for a mixture of squares, triangles, hexagons, and circles for Fractal Dimension might be estimated correctly as 1. But landscapes are limited to a finite number of patches (i.e., samples) on the landscape and it would be difficult to determine how many samples are needed to estimate Fractal Dimension correctly. It has been suggested that 20 patches is the minimum number of samples. However, this number is arbitrary and has no statistical significance.

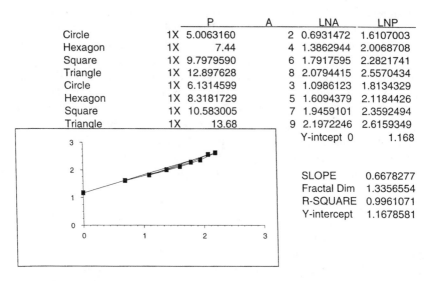

		P	A		LNA	LNP
Circle	1X	5.0063160		2	0.6931472	1.6107003
Hexagon	1X	7.44		4	1.3862944	2.0068708
Square	1X	9.7979590		6	1.7917595	2.2821741
Triangle	1X	12.897628		8	2.0794415	2.5570434
Circle	1X	6.1314599		3	1.0986123	1.8134329
Hexagon	1X	8.3181729		5	1.6094379	2.1184426
Square	1X	10.583005		7	1.9459101	2.3592494
Triangle	1X	13.68		9	2.1972246	2.6159349
					Y-intcept 0	1.168

SLOPE   0.6678277
Fractal Dim   1.3356554
R-SQUARE   0.9961071
Y-intercept   1.1678581

Figure 2.10 *Fractal Dimension* of circles, hexagons, squares, and triangles using perimeter/ area regression at one scale. The slope of the regression is 0.67 which gives a *Fractal Dimension* of 1.34 which according to the *Fractal Dimension* should be 1. Note the high *R²* value of 0.996 which indicates a good fit.

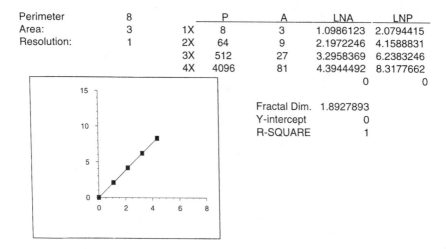

			P	A	LNA	LNP
Perimeter	8	1X	8	3	1.0986123	2.0794415
Area:	3	2X	64	9	2.1972246	4.1588831
Resolution:	1	3X	512	27	3.2958369	6.2383246
		4X	4096	81	4.3944492	8.3177662
					0	0

Fractal Dim.   1.8927893
Y-intercept   0
R-SQUARE   1

Figure 2.11 *Fractal Dimension* of a Sierpinski carpet using perimeter/area regression across scales. The *Fractal Dimension* is 1.8927 which is correct for Sierpinski carpets.

(2) *Raster Data Structures,* Fractal Dimension, *and* SqP

Since there are problems with single-scale perimeter area regression estimation of Fractal Dimension, this section examines the possibility of calculating Fractal Dimension directly from the data. Such a calculation has been proposed by Olsen et al. (1993). Again, this method does not give a true estimate of Fractal Dimension

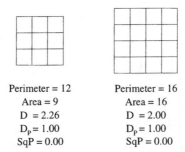

Perimeter = 12   Perimeter = 16
Area = 9   Area = 16
D = 2.26   D = 2.00
D_p = 1.00 D_p = 1.00
SqP = 0.00   SqP = 0.00

Figure 2.12 The perimeter, area, *Fractal Dimension* (D), modified *Fractal Dimension* (D_p), and *SqP* for two different size squares. Notice that the *Fractal Dimension* gives invalid results while the modified *Fractal Dimension* and *SqP* give valid results.

but since Equation 2.7 is an equality, it should be possible to calculate *Fractal Dimension* directly. The general premise is that Fractal Dimension is an equality that can be calculated with the data given. Values for *SqP*, which is derived by direct calculation from the data, are also presented.

In using a raster data structure to represent the landscape, we impose a fixed sampling geometry which limits the possible relationship between perimeter and area. In this section two different equations for calculating *Fractal Dimension* are used. The first equation ignores the constant of proportionality (k) or treats it as an unknown to calculate *Fractal Dimension*:

$$D = 2 * \ln(P)/\ln(A) \qquad (2.10)$$

For perimeter and area values taken from raster data structures this results in *Fractal Dimension* estimates which exceed the legitimate maximum of 2.0 for any object which has greater perimeter than area. In addition, all values are scaled in a manner that is difficult to interpret. These two problems are illustrated in Figure 2.12, where D for the small square is 2.26 and D for a larger square is 2.00. In conventional interpretations of D, the small squares value of 2.26 would be considered representative of a very complex shape. Clearly, a square is not a complex shape. This is why many algorithms for regression estimation delete patches smaller than a threshold number of pixels (normally four pixels). Such elimination often accounts for up to 80% of the data (Hunsaker, 1995, personal communication). As the size of an object increases, the number of pixels making up its area increases exponentially while its perimeter increases more linearly for objects that are not true fractals. Thus, larger patches are much less likely to have a greater number of pixel edges than total number of pixels.

The problem with scaling of D can easily be eliminated if the relationship between perimeter and area in the first equation is expressed using the constant of proportionality as

$$P = kA^{D/2} \qquad (2.11)$$

where $k = 4$ for square pixels.

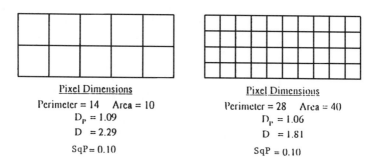

Pixel Dimensions
Perimeter = 14   Area = 10
D_p = 1.09
D = 2.29
SqP = 0.10

Pixel Dimensions
Perimeter = 28   Area = 40
D_p = 1.06
D = 1.81
SqP = 0.10

Figure 2.13   The perimeter, area, modified *Fractal Dimension* (D_p), *Fractal Dimension* (D), and *SqP* values for the same rectangles that differ only in pixel size. D_p decreases slightly as pixel size decreases. D gives invalid results with a large decrease with decreasing pixel size. *SqP* gives the same value for both rectangles.

The value of k is determined by the relationship between perimeter and area for a given geometric shape. When $k = 4$, D can be thought of as the amount the perimeter of a given object that deviates from that of a perfect square of equal area. With D for a square tessellation, we then have

$$D_p = 2 * \ln(P/4)/\ln(A) \qquad (2.12)$$

I have designated this reformulation as D_p. The value of D_p is now constrained to a minimum of 1.0 for any perfect square and cannot exceed 2.0 since the maximum perimeter of a raster object is $4A$ (in pixel units). Equation 2.12 was used by Olsen et al. (1993). The value of k can be replaced for other equilateral tessellations such as hexagons or equilateral triangles.

The results shown in Figure 2.12 suggest that Equation 2.12 represents an accurate method for deriving a *Fractal Dimension*–related complexity metric from a raster image. For example, we now have $D_p = 1.0$ for a square which is a self-similar shape with a topological dimension of 1.0. However, this perimeter-to-area method is not appropriate for other shapes. For example, Figure 2.13 demonstrates that a self-similar rectangle exceeds 1.0 for D_p and decreases with the size of the pixel. As mentioned above, D_p and D measure deviation of the patch shape from an area of some reference geometry. In the case of D_p we are measuring the deviation of perimeter from a perfect square of equivalent area. In the case of D the reference shape is undefined and varies from one case to the next. In order for perimeter to increase in proportion to area as defined in the power law equation of *Fractal Dimension*, the shape of the boundary of a feature must become more complex as area increases. If one simply enlarges an existing shape, perimeter increases linearly while area increases exponentially resulting in confusion between boundary complexity and size for nonfractal geometries.

Thus far, we have not discussed the results of the *SqP*. In Figure 2.12, *SqP* gives expected and consistent results of 0.00 for both squares indicating there is no perimeter deviation from that of a perfect square. *SqP* also gives the same results of 0.10 for the two rectangles in Figure 2.13 indicating a slight perimeter deviation from that of a perfect square. *SqP* performs much better than D and D_p in both cases.

(3) *Measurement Resolution,* Fractal Dimension, *and* SqP

In order for a complexity metric to be most useful, it is important that it be predictable with measurement resolution. This would allow comparison of complexity of landscapes at different spatial resolutions and enhance comparisons across different study areas and time periods. For example, a landscape sampled using Landsat TM data at 30-m resolution and Landsat MSS data at 79-m resolution should have similar complexity dimensions. Most of the methods used for calculating *Fractal Dimension* base the measurement resolution for perimeter and area on the assumption of a pixel of unit size. This assumption is invalid for both fractal and nonfractal objects. Perimeter and area are not linearly related. Given an object sampled at two different spatial resolutions, the resulting *Fractal Dimension* values can be different and unpredictable.

This relationship is demonstrated by referring back to Figure 2.13, where the rectangle on the left is initially sampled at a coarse resolution and then duplicated at a finer resolution by doubling the sampling rate. Here, D_p changes between the two rectangles solely on the assumption that pixel size does not matter. This decrease occurs when pixels are used as the unit of measurement because the number of within-patch pixels increases at an exponential rate while the number of edge pixels increases at a linear rate. This resulting reduction in perimeter/area ratio decreases the estimate of Fractal Dimension.

This problem doesn't arise when perimeter and area are calculated using an absolute measurement scale. *SqP* handles the problem by taking the square root of area so that the rate of increase or decrease in pixels does not become a problem. Figure 2.13 shows that for *SqP* the same value of 0.10 was determined for both rectangles.

The strength of the aforementioned phenomenon was tested on three landscapes in Figure 2.14: Santa Barbara, Goleta, and Bakersfield, California. In all three cases, *Fractal Dimension* estimated by regression decreased after replicating pixels on the image. *Fractal Dimension* then remained stable following further pixel replications. The phenomena appeared inexplicable at first look until another problem with *Fractal Dimension* was discovered. In calculating *Fractal Dimension* using regression, as mentioned earlier, patches with pixels fewer than four are eliminated from the analysis. When pixel numbers are multiplied by two per side, all one-cell patches become four-cell patches which are then included in the regression estimation and *Fractal Dimension* changes. Beyond that, since there are no data eliminated nor added in the analysis in further replications, the *Fractal Dimension* remains the same as the first pixel replication. *SqP*, on the other hand, remained constant throughout all replications. Since all the data are included and normalized in the calculation of *SqP*, there were no changes in its value due to pixel replication.

(4) *Shape Complexity,* Fractal Dimension, *and* SqP

We have thus far shown the problems with *Fractal Dimension* for geometric and even fractal shapes and how *SqP* alleviates these problems. But what about other

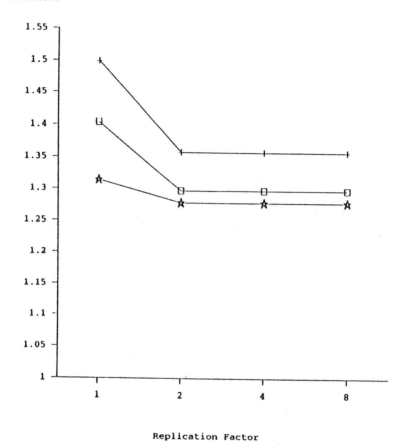

Fractal Dimension

Figure 2.14   The effects of pixel replication on the value of *Fractal Dimension* for three California landscapes: Santa Barbara (top); Goleta (middle); and Bakersfield (bottom). All three show the same pattern. *Fractal Dimension* decreases after a replication of two and then remains constant following further replications.

shapes? I conclude this chapter by presenting the two shapes in Figure 2.15: a cross and two connecting crosses. The traditional *Fractal Dimension D* gives invalid numbers and recognizes the shape on the left as being more complex than the one on the right. The modified *Fractal Dimension D_p* gives more reasonable results and recognizes the shape on the right as slightly more complex than the one on the left. *SqP* gives valid results and recognizes the shape on the right as much more complex than the shape on the left.

The chapters that follow will empirically show how the improved metrics of *PPU* and *SqP* can correct for problems identified with *Contagion* and *Fractal Dimension*. And how, by being more robust, metrics can be expanded to a variety of future uses.

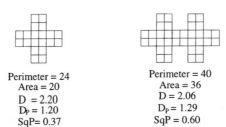

Perimeter = 24
Area = 20
D = 2.20
D_P = 1.20
SqP= 0.37

Perimeter = 40
Area = 36
D = 2.06
D_P = 1.29
SqP = 0.60

Figure 2.15 The perimeter, area, *Fractal Dimension* (*D*), modified *Fractal Dimension* (*D*$_p$), and *SqP* for two different shapes. Notice that the *Fractal Dimension* gives invalid results and indicates that the shape on the left is more complex than the shape on the right. The modified *Fractal Dimension* gives valid results and indicates that the shape on the right is slightly more complex than the shape on the left. *SqP* also gives valid results and indicates the shape on the right as clearly more complex than the shape on the left.

CHAPTER **3**

Research Methods

Because of the problems found with *Contagion* and *Fractal Dimension*, improved landscape ecology metrics were developed. In order to determine whether or not the improved metrics were sensitive to landscape pattern and were predictable with changes in spatial resolution, a rigorous empirical analysis of all four metrics was performed. The *PPU* was compared with *Contagion* and the *SqP* was compared with *Fractal Dimension* for four different landscapes with various gradients of change.

3.1 OVERVIEW OF EXPERIMENTAL DESIGN

An overview of the methodology employed in this research is presented in Figure 3.1. The left side of the flowchart depicts the systematic evaluation of the landscape metrics. The right side of the flowchart outlines the empirical steps in the experimental design. In this research two types of tests were primarily employed to determine (1) if the metrics were capable of distinguishing between landscape pattern along predictable gradients and (2) if the metrics were insensitive or gave consistent results when the data were manipulated to change spatial resolution.

Empirical analysis of the landscape metrics involved a number of steps. Landsat images were acquired and classified using a variety of methods depending on the study site, availability of ancillary data, and level of classification. The most common method used was an iterative self-organizing clustering algorithm (ERDAS ISOCLAS). The number of clusters and path iterations was based on image variance and the classification scheme. Clusters were then labeled to appropriate landcover classes, depending on the study site, based on visual inspection and interpretation of the imagery. The results were GIS files identifying landcover types for different areas and, in some cases, different time periods. More detail on the classification schemes used is provided for each study site in later sections.

Once the images were classified, landscape metrics were calculated on each GIS file. *Contagion*, *Fractal Dimension*, *PPU*, and *SqP* were calculated using a C program. After the initial values of the landscape metrics were determined, the

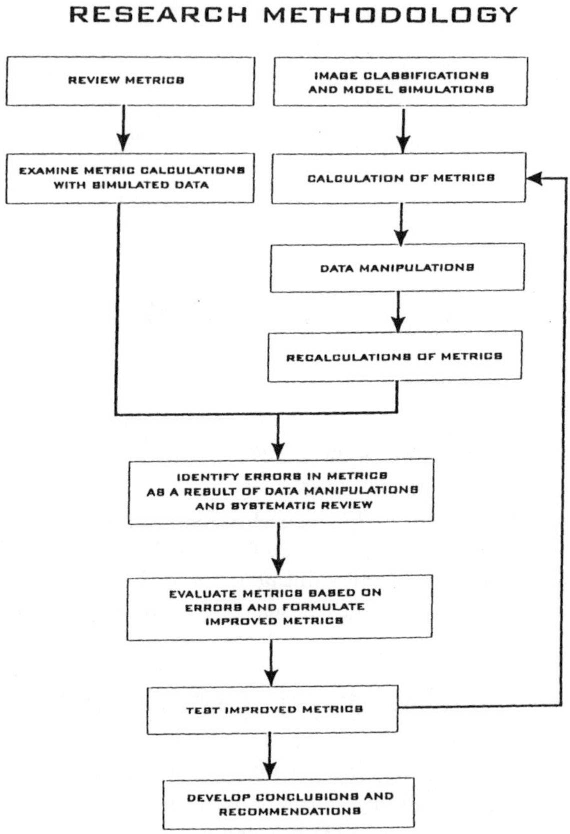

RESEARCH METHODOLOGY

Figure 3.1 Flowchart showing the methodology of this research.

GIS files were subjected to a series of data manipulations in order to vary their base spatial resolution. To study the effects of spatial resolution, image classifications for the various study areas were resampled using a majority filter at successively coarser intervals of 60 m up to a nominal resolution of 1 km. This 1 km maximum level of aggregation was selected to correspond generally with AVHRR local area coverage (LAC) data which is often used in studies of tropical deforestation (e.g., Malingreau and Tucker, 1988) and global classification schemes. Aggregation involved using an increasing size majority filter on the original GIS classified image (e.g., 3 × 3, 5 × 5, 7 × 7, etc.).

Landscape metrics were calculated for each aggregation. At the finest scales of aggregation, rapid unpredictable changes in a metric would suggest the degree to which image data might be producing biased estimates of the landcover types. This assessment was made, for example, in the context of mixing Landsat TM and Landsat MSS data in a historical study of land-use change in the Amazon. Such cross-sensor comparisons are likely to become more common, as MSS data has the longest historical record but is no longer acquired in some areas of the Amazon. At coarser levels of aggregation, the utility of coarse resolution sensors for capturing landcover patterns was tested.

A basic hypothesis of this research was that both *Contagion* and *Fractal Dimension* would be sensitive to measurement resolution. It was also hypothesized that the improved metrics, developed as part of this research, would compensate for the errors determined from measurement resolution manipulations of the data. In addition, it was hypothesized that these improved metrics would give consistent and predictable results.

3.2 CAPABILITY OF METRICS TO CAPTURE CHANGES IN LANDSCAPE PATTERN

To address the capability of the landscape metrics to detect changes in landscape pattern, a general model of landcover change was developed for each study area. For example, for the Sierra Nevada study site, low values were predicted for shape complexity and fragmentation for large agricultural areas; and high values for shape complexity and fragmentation for urban and natural categories such as forest and chaparral. For each study site a model of spatial pattern was developed and is shown and described below. The expected models were then compared to the observed values for each of the study sites to determine if metrics under investigation were behaving in the expected manner.

It should be pointed out that actual metric values for the landcovers under investigation could not be predicted due to the lack of empirical research for land-cover type values of these metrics. Only general trends in landscape pattern were explored. However, for each study site, the coefficient of variation (standard deviation of metric values divided by the mean of metric values) was used as a diagnostic for quantitative comparison between landscape metrics.

3.3 SENSITIVITY OF METRICS TO SPATIAL RESOLUTION OF REMOTE SENSING DATA

Landscape metrics were calculated for each aggregation. Each metric was then evaluated by comparing values between data before and after data manipulation. The metrics were evaluated qualitatively by plotting metric values and visually inspecting spatial resolution changes in those values. For each metric and study site a regression model was developed for the aggregated data. It was hypothesized that the regression model would indicate consistent and predictable results for the improved metrics and inconsistent, unpredictable results for the traditional metrics. If the improved landscape metrics gave a quantitative predictable response due to a regression equation, then data at different spatial resolutions could be calibrated for comparison in future studies. Such comparison would be very important in studies that use finer resolution data to evaluate the capability of coarse resolution data, such as using Landsat TM 30-m data with NOAA AVHRR 1.1-km data for detecting and validating global landcover changes.

3.4 ANALYSIS OF METRICS ALONG A SPATIAL GRADIENT IN RONDÔNIA, BRAZIL

The Rondônia, Brazil study site is located in the south-central portion of the Amazon Basin of Brazil (Figure 3.2). One Landsat TM scene for 1986 was acquired for the area. The scene was classified into two categories: forest and cleared (generally clearing for practicing agriculture). Ten 512 × 512 subscenes were sampled from this image. The subscenes were systematically sampled at 5-km intervals so that each scene became farther away from the major urban center. The expected model in using these subscenes was that the farther away the location of the site from the urban center (located at the bottom right of the scene), the lower the deforestation and higher the amount of forest. Fragmentation was predicted to increase for each subscene as the location was closer to the urban center.

Shape complexity should increase as the homogeneous forest becomes increasingly filled with small rectilinear settlements as the study site is located closer to the urban center. The shape complexity should reach an asymptote as the cleared area becomes greater than the forested area, at which point the shape complexity should decline. The expected model is shown in Figure 3.3.

3.5 ANALYSIS OF METRICS ALONG A SPATIAL GRADIENT IN WASHINGTON, D.C.

The study site is located northwest of Washington, D.C. with Frederick, Maryland in the north, Leesburg, Virginia in the southwest, and Gaithersburg, Maryland in the southeast (Plate 1*). The landscape is dominated by grassland and cropland. Most of the grassland is composed of either dairy farms or suburban lawns. Deciduous forest is found around areas that are not well suited for agriculture or dairy production. This is evident in riparian areas, parklands, and areas of high slope and elevation, such as Catoctin Mountain in the western portion of the image and Sugarloaf Mountain which is located near the center of the map just east of the Monocacy River. Evergreen forest and shrub lands appear in small patches throughout the map. Water tends to be rather concentrated, as would be expected, with the Potomac River running through the southwest portion of the map, the Monocacy River running from Frederick to the Potomac, and Black Hills Reservoir just northwest of Gaithersburg. Wetlands appear in areas around tributaries, especially around the two major rivers. Even though there is a large amount of natural vegetation, there are several urbanized areas that are growing at a rapid rate. This is especially evident along the Interstate 270 corridor between Gaithersburg and Frederick and the Route 7 corridor that leads from Leesburg into Washington, D.C.

The base map used in this study was produced as a part of the NOAA CoastWatch Change Analysis Project (C-CAP) Chesapeake Bay prototype. The map was classified from Landsat TM imagery that was acquired on October 12, 1989. According to Congalton et al. (1994), the database has an overall accuracy of approximately 68%.

---

* Plate 1 appears following page 50.

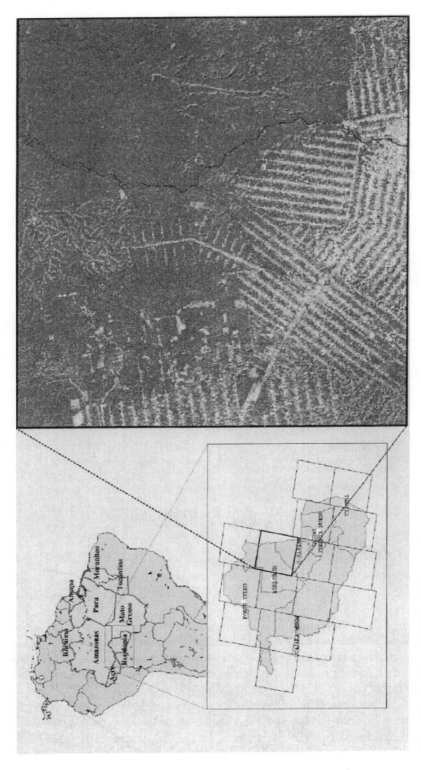

Figure 3.2 Location of the Rondônia study site.

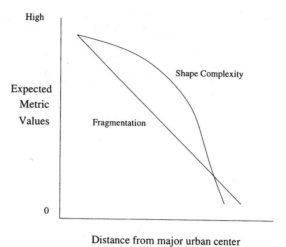

Figure 3.3   The expected behavior of the landscape metrics as a function of distance from major urban center for the Rondônia study site.

Table 3.1   The IGBP and C-CAP Landcover Classes for the Washington, D.C. Study Area

IGBP Landcover Classes	C-Cap Landcover Classes
Evergreen needle leaf forest	Evergreen forest
Deciduous broadleaf forest	Deciduous forest
Mixed forest	Mixed forest
Shrub lands	Mixed shrub/scrub mixed
	Scrub/shrub
Grasslands	Grasslands
Wetlands	Palustrine forest
	Estuarine emergent wetlands
	Palustrine emergent wetland
Croplands	Cropland
Urban	High-intensity developed
	Low-intensity developed
Water	Water

The classification scheme used in this map is the standard C-CAP protocol classification that consists of 14 classes (Dobson, 1992). The study area was 1250 × 1250 pixels.

The C-CAP data were reclassified to its approximate class most equivalent to the International Geosphere Biosphere Program (IGBP) classification scheme. The IGBP classification scheme has 17 different classes (Belward and Loveland, 1995). Evergreen broadleaf forests, deciduous needle leaf forests, woody savannas, savannas, and barrens were not included in this study since they were not characteristic of this area. Cropland/natural vegetation mosaics were not included since they were not represented at the 30-m resolution. Closed shrub lands and open shrub lands had to be merged into a single shrub lands category since the C-CAP data did not differentiate between the two. Table 3.1 shows the reclassification scheme used to create the comparable IGBP classes from the C-CAP data set. Even though this

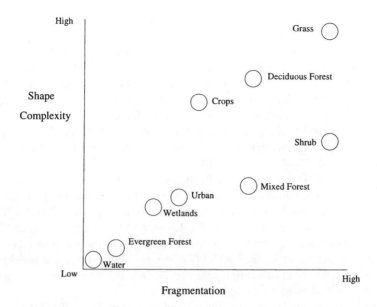

Figure 3.4 The expected model for metric behavior with respect to landcover types for the Washington, D.C. area study site.

method gives an approximation of the IGBP classes, it was decided that the time and resources saved by using the C-CAP data set outweighed the advantages of deriving an IGBP landcover map directly from Landsat TM data.

The expected model for the Washington, D.C. area is quite complex (Figure 3.4). Grassland and shrub land appear to be the most fragmented, while water and evergreen forest appear on the map to be the most contagiously arranged. The urban category also appears to be less fragmented than one would expect. Perhaps there is a transition from suburban to urban for metropolitan areas where the patches become more homogeneous. Croplands appear more fragmented than urban which is unusual. This pattern could possibly be due to the legacy of the old Virginia Military District cadastral system of the area. Croplands also appear to be more complex than urban areas. Deciduous forest and grassland boundaries appear the most complex, while water and evergreen forest appear the least complex.

3.6 ANALYSIS OF METRICS ALONG A VERTICAL GRADIENT IN THE SIERRA NEVADA

The Sierra Nevada is a unified mountain range that extends about 570 km from Lassen Peak at the north to the edge of Walker Pass, east of Bakersfield, California. A Landsat TM scene that covered the study area for August 25, 1990 (path 42, row 35) was acquired from the University of California at Santa Barbara Map and Imagery Library (MIL) (Plate 2*). The scene represents the driest month of the year

---

* Plate 2 appears following page 50.

which allows for good visual differentiation between vegetation areas and has minimal snow coverage in the alpine regions.

The Landsat scene was geometrically corrected and projected in the UTM coordinate system to allow a direct comparison with the natural vegetation map of California (CALVEG, 1991). The CALVEG map was rasterized to a nominal spatial resolution of 30 m to aid in the geometric correction and comparison. The Landsat image was then classified into binary GIS files for each of the following seven categories: (1) alpine (Alp); (2) forest (For); (3) chaparral (Cha); (4) small agricultural fields (Ags); (5) medium-sized agricultural fields (Agm); (6) large agricultural fields (Agl); and (7) urban areas (Urb).

The binary files were created so the individual landscape metric values could be calculated for each landcover type. The classification scheme for each landcover involved an iterative self-organizing clustering algorithm (ERDAS ISOCLAS) specifying 16 clusters and five iteration paths. Landsat TM channels 3, 4, 5, and 7 were used for the unsupervised classification. The number of clusters was based on image variance, comparisons with the CALVEG map, field observations, and consideration of the simple binary classification scheme. The results were seven classified GIS files for each landcover category.

The expected model for the seven landcover classes in the Sierra Nevada describes a strong differentiation between natural and anthropogenic categories (Figure 3.5). The urban category should have the highest shape complexity since it consists of a mixture of roads, residential areas, business, and industrial areas. The urban area is more fragmented with respect to the other six categories and should show the highest fragmentation values. The natural categories of forest and chaparral should have the next highest perimeter-to-area ratios and thus the highest shape complexity. The urban, chaparral, and alpine areas show relatively little fragmentation and should have much lower fragmentation values than the urban category. The agricultural areas should have the least shape complexity and fragmentation since they consist of simple-shaped square and rectangular fields which are relatively homogeneous and unfragmented.

3.7 ANALYSIS OF METRICS ALONG A TEMPORAL GRADIENT IN OURO PRÊTO, BRAZIL

For the temporal gradient study site, Landsat MSS and TM imagery were used along with a socioeconomic model of land-use change (called DELTA) of Ouro Prêto, Brazil.

A comparison of image data and the DELTA (Dynamic Ecological Land Tenure Analysis) model was performed on a sample of 294 lots in the Ouro Prêto colonization area of Rondônia. The Ouro Prêto colonization project was the first of 16 old, new, and planned colonization projects in Rondônia (Figure 3.6). The Ouro Prêto colonization project began in 1970 and occupies an area over 5100 km². Road building began in Ouro Prêto in 1972, enabling the tropical forests to be cleared for agriculture. Farmers settled on 100-ha lots which were laid out systematically along the road network at 4 to 5 km spacings (Frohn et al., 1990). The project had settled 4000 families by 1974 (Mueller, 1980) and 5098 families by 1987 (Becker, 1987; Millikan, 1988).

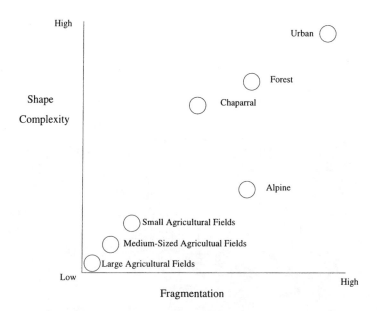

Figure 3.5   The expected model for metric behavior with respect to landcover types for the Sierra Nevada study site.

The 294 lot samples in Ouro Prêto were located 50 to 70 km from the market center of Ouro Prêto d'Oeste and the only paved highway through Rondônia (BR-364). While colonists began settling near this market center of Ouro Prêto in 1972, it was estimated from Landsat MSS images that colonists began settling in the study area covering the 294 lot sample in 1977. The lot sizes in this area range from 53 to 120 ha with an average lot size of 101 ha.

Landsat data covering the area of the 294 sample lots in Ouro Prêto were acquired for five time periods 1973, 1976, 1978, 1980 (MSS), and 1986 (TM). Since there was no detectable activity in the 294 lot area until 1977, only the 1978, 1980, and 1986 data could be used for this analysis. The data were first coregistered to a digitized blueprint map of roads and lot boundaries for the area. Areas outside of the 294 lot study area were masked from each scene. Images were then classified into forested and cleared areas using iterative self-organizing clustering algorithm (ERDAS ISOCLAS) and specifying 15 clusters. The number of clusters was based on image variance and the simple binary classification scheme. Clusters were then labeled based on visual inspection of the imagery. This resulted in three GIS files identifying forest and cleared areas for 1978, 1980, and 1986.

The DELTA model was developed to simulate the spatial effects of colonization and road development on land-use change (Southworth et al., 1991; Dale et al., 1993a). DELTA is a stochastic, dynamic, microsimulation model that integrates three submodels which simulate settlement diffusion, land-use change, and ecological change. The model can estimate patterns and rates of deforestation under different immigration policies, land tenure practices, and road development scenarios.

The ecological effects within the integrated model are evaluated at the aggregate, regionwide level while the dynamics of land-use pattern formation are simulated at

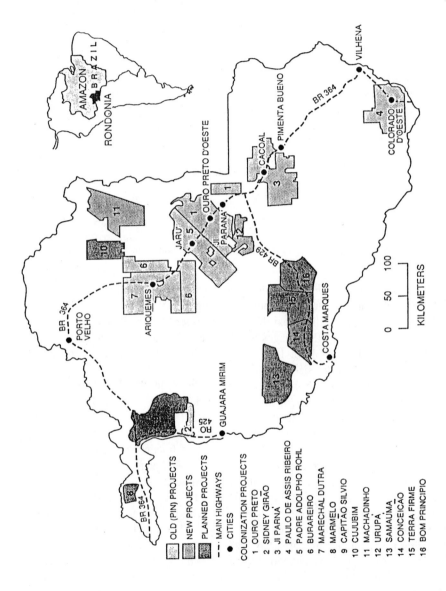

Figure 3.6 Location of the Ouro Prêto study site.

the individual lot level. The model tracks the land-use and migrant status of each lot over a period of years. The model also tracks the history of the colonists on the land so that the resulting aggregate patterns of land-use change reflect the human settlement process. Selection of a particular lot for settlement is based upon lot size, three indexes of agricultural suitability (based on soil quality and physical aspect), distance to nearest market along paved and feeder roads, and the length of an occupant's current tenure. As part of the simulation, colonists leaving a lot either occupy a new lot, emigrate from the area, or become part of the local labor pool of landless workers. Lots can also be coalesced into larger holdings or disaggregated.

The model uses both spatial and nonspatial data as inputs. Spatial data include lot size, location with respect to neighboring lots, distance to market and to primary and feeder roads, soil conditions, and original vegetation types. Road data, lot boundaries, agricultural and pasture suitability, and vegetation have been entered into a GIS that interfaces with the model. As the model is run, data on the land-use history are recorded for each lot every year. Nonspatial inputs include lot occupancy decisions, conditions for coalescing or disaggregating lots, criteria for a tenant's change in farming practices, and choice variables for tenants abandoning a lot and moving elsewhere. Stochastic elements are also introduced into many of the lot selection and land-use decisions to allow a realistic simulation by averaging over multiple computer runs, for a single set of parameter inputs. The model projects both the changes over time in the area and the spatial arrangement of landcover types. For additional information on the DELTA model and its capabilities, see Southworth et al., 1991, and Dale et al., 1993a and b, and 1994.

The DELTA model was applied to the 294 lot sample area of Ouro Prêto over a 20-year time period. Model parameters simulated colonists in Rondônia who cut trees from about 3 ha per year, burn them, plant annual and perennial crops, and turn the land into pasture as the soil degrades (Leite and Furley, 1985; Millikan, 1988). Model projections capture the major features of farmers in central Rondônia as determined by comparison with data from interviews with farmers (Dale et al., 1993b). A comparison of the DELTA model output and the classification of Landsat data for 1978, 1980, and 1986 is provided in Figure 3.7. The model approach shows less spatial heterogeneity since clearing is modeled at the lot level rather than at the pixel level. Thus, the model ignores considerations such as obstacles to farming within a lot (e.g., ponds, ditches, or mounds).

The expected temporal model for Ouro Prêto should exhibit the following trends. Initially, the fragmentation should be low since the landscape is dominated by one large homogeneous patch of forest (Figure 3.8). As settlers move into the area, fragmentation should increase as the forest becomes fragmented by deforested lots for agriculture. As more and more settlers enter the area and clear more forest, the fragmentation should reach an asymptote where forest and deforestation are nearly equal in proportion. At this point, fragmentation should decrease as the area becomes dominated by large patches of deforestation. For shape complexity, a similar trend was expected. Initially, the area is one large square patch of forest. As settlers move in, the landscape becomes more complex until it reaches an asymptote, at which point shape complexity should drop as the forest becomes dominated by simple-shaped square and rectangular fields.

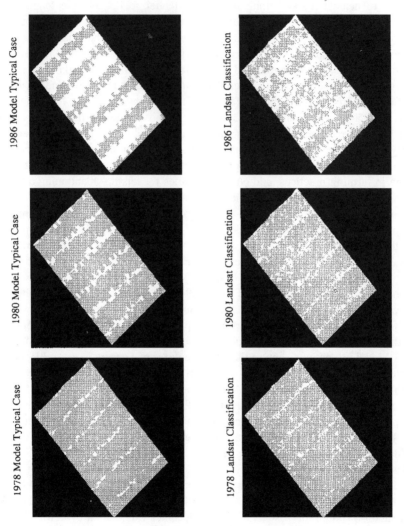

Figure 3.7 Landsat classifications and DELTA model simulations for 1978, 1980, and 1986.

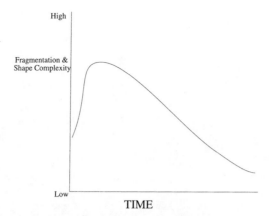

Figure 3.8 Expected temporal trends in fragmentation and shape complexity for the Ouro Prêto study site. Note that both fragmentation and shape complexity should exhibit similar if not the same trends.

CHAPTER 4

Empirical Analysis of Landscape Metrics

The goal of this research was to develop and test improved metrics for landscape analysis. In the preceding chapter, the methodology in achieving this goal was documented. This chapter presents the results and discussion of the analyses of the improved and traditional landscape metrics on the various study sites

4.1 METRIC CAPABILITY IN QUANTIFYING CHANGES ALONG A SPATIAL GRADIENT IN RONDÔNIA, BRAZIL

Results of the amount of forest cleared as a function of the distance of a study area from a major urban center are shown in Figure 4.1. Results indicated that the farther away the study area from the urban center, the lower the amount of deforested area. The relationship shows a near linear negative correlation between distance and clearing with each 5-km interval. The explanation appears straightforward. Farmers settle closer to major urban centers to allow easier access for the transport of goods and services to and from markets in the urban center.

4.1.1 Sensitivity of Metrics to Landscape Pattern Variation

Figure 4.2 shows the results for *Contagion* and *PPU* with respect to distance from the major urban center. Although *Contagion* shows an overall increase with respect to distance, it initially shows a decrease until a distance of 20 km is reached. This distance of 20 km was where the study areas move away from the major highway of BR-364. The reason for the initial decrease, which would indicate that clumping is decreasing as the area is located farther from the urban center, is the within-patch pixel problem of *Contagion*. Initially, areas closer to the urban center have larger patches with a higher ratio of within-patch pixels to edge pixels. As study areas were located farther away from the urban center, the ratio of within-patch pixels to edge pixels decreases and *Contagion* decreases. *Contagion* finally begins to increase as the fish bone fragmentation pattern areas contain no large

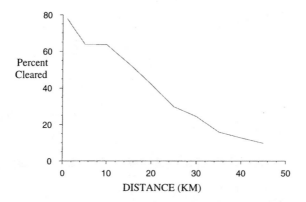

Figure 4.1 Changes in the amount of forest cleared as a result of distance from major urban center. Graph shows that as distance from a major urban center increases the amount of cleared forest decreases.

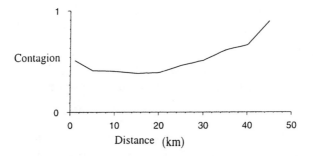

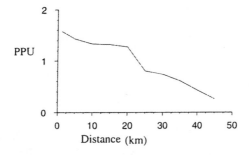

Figure 4.2 Changes in the values of *Contagion* and *PPU* as a result of changes in distance from a major urban center. *Contagion* initially decreases until a distance of 20 km is reached, at which point it increases. *PPU* decreases continuously as distance increases. *PPU* shows a sharp decrease when a distance of 20 km is reached.

patches and the within-patch pixel problem has little effect. This effect can be viewed more easily by examining the images of the ten study areas themselves in Figures 4.3 to 4.12.

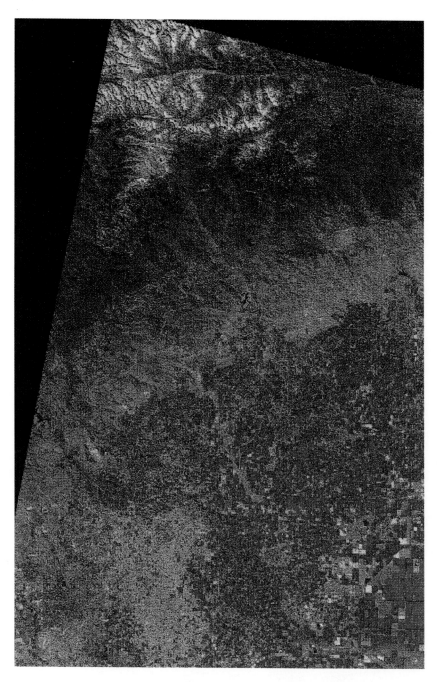

Plate 1. Washington, D.C. Study Site: 30-meter resolution.

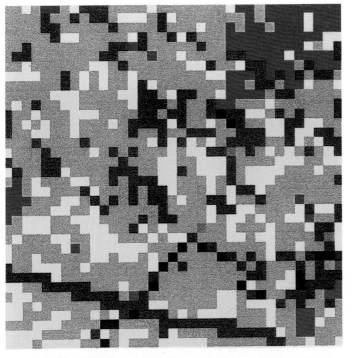

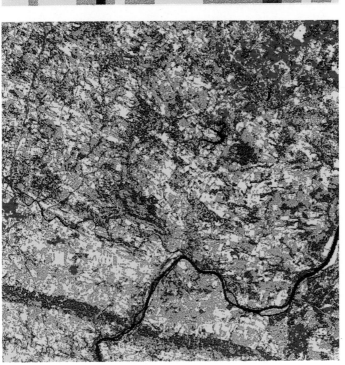

Plate 2. Landsat TM False Color IR Image of the Sierra Nevada study site.

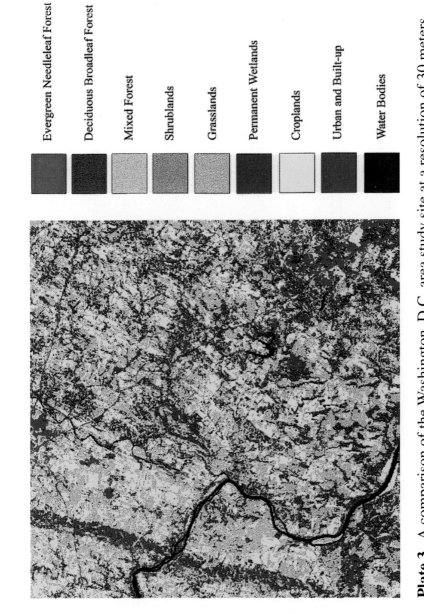

Evergreen Needleleaf Forest

Deciduous Broadleaf Forest

Mixed Forest

Shrublands

Grasslands

Permanent Wetlands

Croplands

Urban and Built-up

Water Bodies

Plate 3. A comparison of the Washington, D.C. area study site at a resolution of 30 meters (left) and 1050 meters (right).

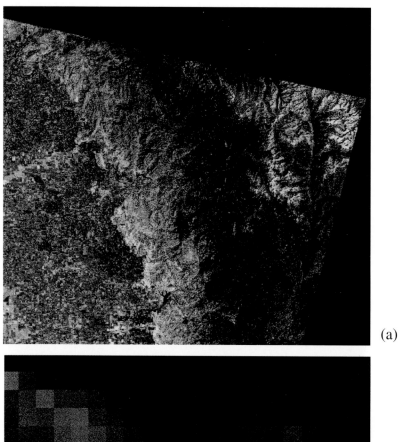

(a)

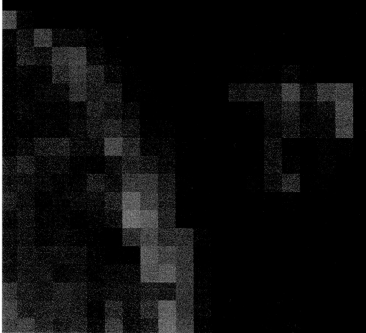

(b)

Plate 4. (a) The Sierra Nevada study site at a spatial resolution of 30 meters. (b) The Sierra Nevada study site at
a spatialresolution of 1050 meters.

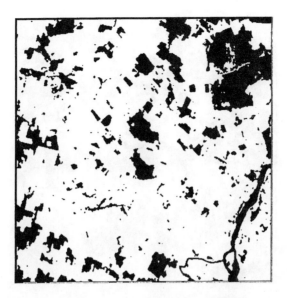

Figure 4.3 Locations of a study area 1 km from an urban center. The area consists mostly of clearing and is fragmented by isolated patches of forest.

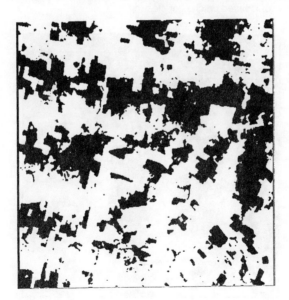

Figure 4.4 Location of a study area 5 km from an urban center. The area consists mostly of clearing and is fragmented by isolated patches of forest and a small number of isolated patches of clearing.

PPU does not exhibit this problem and shows a predicted and continuous decline. In this respect, *PPU* behaves in a consistent manner with that exhibited by fragmentation as the study areas are located farther from the urban center. Notice that at 20 km, *PPU* shows a sharp decline. Again, this is due to the location of the study

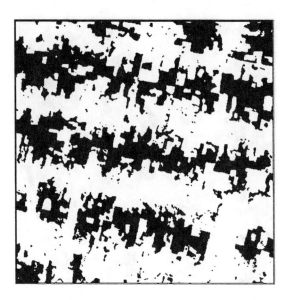

Figure 4.5 Location of a study area 10 km from an urban center. The area consists mostly of clearing and is fragmented by isolated patches of forest and an increasing number of isolated patches of clearing.

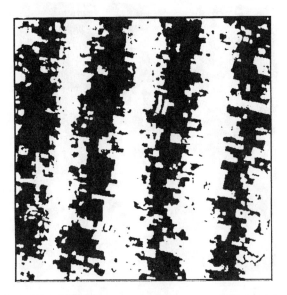

Figure 4.6 Location of a study area 15 km from an urban center. The area consists mostly of clearing and is fragmented by isolated patches of forest and an increased number of isolated patches of clearing.

areas farther away from Highway BR-364. This sharp decline demonstrates the sensitivity of *PPU* to sudden changes in landscape pattern. The coefficients of variation for *PPU* and *Contagion* were 0.417 and 0.314, respectively, which indicates that *PPU* again was more sensitive to changes in landscape pattern. However, this

Figure 4.7 Location of a study area 20 km from an urban center. The area consists of nearly an equal amount of clearing and forest. The area is fragmented by an equal number of isolated forest and cleared patches.

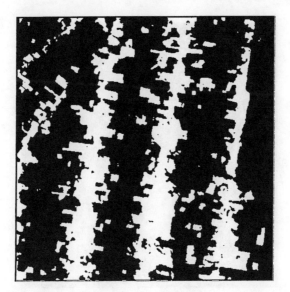

Figure 4.8 Location of a study area 25 km from an urban center. The area is dominated by homogeneous forest patches. The cleared patches are more contiguous and less fragmented.

diagnostic is not as important, in this case, since the *Contagion* pattern shows counterintuitive results unlike those derived from *PPU*.

Changes in the values of *Fractal Dimension* and *SqP* are shown in Figure 4.13. *Fractal Dimension* shows no distinct pattern with varying peaks and valleys.

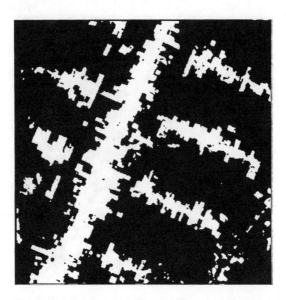

Figure 4.9   Location of a study area 30 km from an urban center. The area is dominated by homogeneous forest patches. The area is fragmented by large contiguous patches of cleared areas.

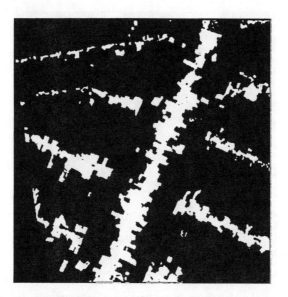

Figure 4.10   Location of a study area 35 km from an urban center. The area is dominated by homogeneous forest patches. The area is fragmented by fewer contiguous patches of cleared areas.

No general conclusions can be derived from its graph other than that its measure of shape complexity as a function of distance is nonpredictable. The varying *Fractal Dimension* patterns are most probably due to the various errors in using linear regression for estimating *Fractal Dimension*, as discussed in Chapter 2.

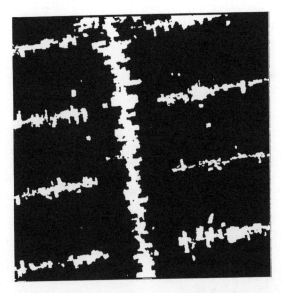

Figure 4.11 Location of a study area 40 km from an urban center. The area is dominated by forest. The area is fragmented by several thin contiguous patches of cleared areas.

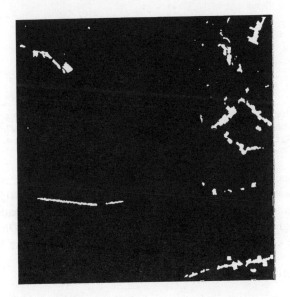

Figure 4.12 Location of a study area 45 km from an urban center. The area is almost completely dominated by forest with a few isolated patches of clearing.

SqP, on the other hand, shows a distinct pattern. Shape complexity decreases sharply from a distance of 20 km. The pattern is reasonable. Shape complexity is low when there are few rectangular patches on the landscape. As patches coalesce and road networks form, the SqP values increase. Complexity reaches a maximum at 20 km, where the study areas reach the major Highway BR-364. Between 1 and

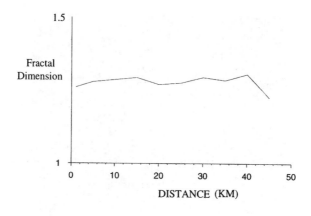

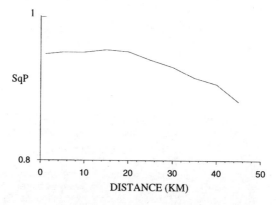

Figure 4.13 Changes in the values of *Fractal Dimension* and *SqP* with distance from a major urban center. *Fractal Dimension* shows an increase followed by peaks and valleys. *SqP* shows little change until a distance of 20 km is reached, at which point *SqP* shows a steady decrease.

20 km, the shape complexity of the landscape as determined by *SqP* remains similar. The coefficients of variation for *SqP* and *Fractal Dimension* were 0.258 and 0.017, respectively, indicating that *SqP* is more sensitive to changes in pattern. Although, again, this diagnostic is not as important as the fact that *Fractal Dimension* shows no explainable complexity pattern as a function of distance, unlike *SqP*.

4.1.2 Sensitivity of Metrics to Spatial Resolution

The effects of varying spatial resolution on the values of *Contagion* and *PPU* are shown in Figure 4.14. Both appear to decline logarithmically as pixel size increases. This decline is counterintuitive for *Contagion* because the *Contagion* values should increase since aggregation causes less fragmentation and more clumping (see Figure 4.15a and 4.15b). The reason for the seemingly counterintuitive decline appears to be the within-patch pixel problem described in Chapter 2. With

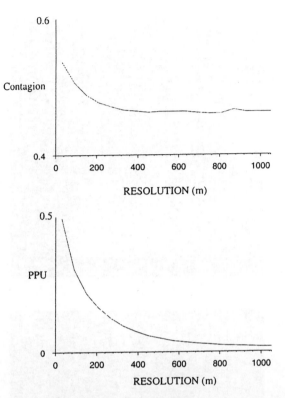

Figure 4.14 The result of changing spatial resolution on the values of *Contagion* and *PPU* is shown in these two graphs. As resolution becomes larger, *Contagion* decreases, contrary to theory. *PPU* shows a logarithmic continuous decline with increasing resolution.

each aggregation, within-patch pixels decrease at a greater rate than edge pixels which causes the value of *Contagion* to decline. Thus, even though the landscape has become more clumped and less fragmented, the pixel adjacency problem causes *Contagion* values to decline in an unexpected manner.

PPU, on the other hand, shows a predictable response with each aggregation. As the landscape becomes more clumped and less fragmented, *PPU* declines. The pattern is a smooth logarithmic decrease with each aggregation. In order to examine the logarithmic relationship between *PPU* and spatial resolution, regression analysis was performed on *PPU* and spatial resolution. The log of *PPU* was plotted against the log of spatial resolution and linear regression was determined from the fitted line. The result of the plot is depicted in Figure 4.16 which shows a near linear fit with an R^2 value of 0.95. The regression equation is

$$\log\left(P_{size}\right) = -0.892\left(\log(PPU)\right) + 1.500$$

where P_{size} is the length of the side of a square pixel in meters. This equation was tested by using Landsat MSS (79 m) data for the same date and area as the Landsat

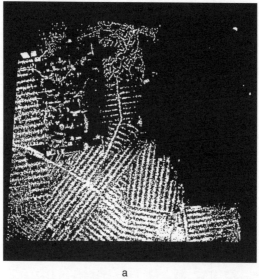

a

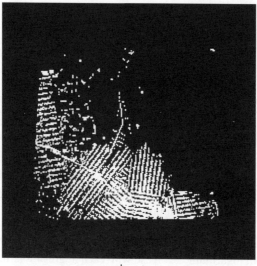

b

Figure 4.15   (a) Classified Landsat TM image of forest (black) and clearings (white) at 30 m for Rondônia. (b) Classified Landsat TM image of forest (black) and clearings (white) aggregated to 1050 m for Rondônia.

(30 m) to determine if the expected and observed values were similar for *PPU*. The results are generally consistent and presented later.

The result of changing spatial resolution on *Fractal Dimension* and the *SqP* metrics are shown in Figure 4.17. The plot for *Fractal Dimension* shows a jagged overall increase in values from 30 to 1050 m. This increase is counterintuitive since the result of aggregation creates a smoother, less-complex landscape. Others have

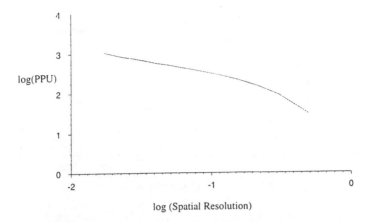

Figure 4.16 Log/log regression plot of *PPU* vs. spatial resolution. As seen above, the plot shows a near linear fit after the log/log transformations.

found similar results with *Fractal Dimension* and spatial resolution (Kienast, 1993; Benson and Mackenzie, 1995). *Fractal Dimension* would indicate that shape complexity increases as the landscape becomes more generalized. The reason for the increases in *Fractal Dimension* is problems with linear regression in estimating its value. One cannot pinpoint which problems are occurring, whether they may be faulty y-intercepts, spread of data values, or incorrect fits. The list is numerous and unpredictable, as there are many peaks and valleys in the *Fractal Dimension* plot. The general conclusion is that *Fractal Dimension* gives unpredictable results as spatial resolution varies.

The opposite is true for *SqP*. *SqP* shows a steady linear decrease with each aggregation. As the landscape becomes more generalized and less complex, *SqP* is sensitive to these changes and gives a predictable response. Linear regression was performed to determine the correlation between *SqP* and spatial resolution. Regression resulted in a nearly perfect linear fit with an R^2 value of 0.997. The regression equation for *SqP* with respect to spatial resolution was

$$P_{\text{size}} = -27958.47(SqP) + 27699.451$$

This equation was also tested using Landsat MSS 79-m data to determine if the expected and observed values were similar. The results suggest that the regression equation is adequate in predicting values at different spatial resolutions and are discussed below.

4.1.3 Test of the Regression Equations for *PPU* and *SqP* Using Landsat MSS 79-m Data

The purpose of this analysis was to determine if the regression equations previously derived are valid with data of different spatial resolutions. In this case, we are not only comparing differing spatial resolutions but different sensors as well.

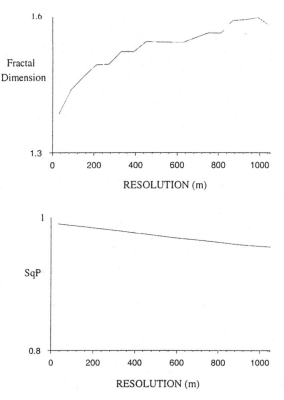

Figure 4.17 The result of changing spatial resolution on the values of *Fractal Dimension* and *SqP*. *Fractal Dimension* exhibits an overall jagged increase with resolution, contrary to theory. *SqP*, on the other hand, shows a continuous linear decrease with resolution.

Landsat MSS 79-m was acquired for the same area and time period as the Landsat TM 30-m data. The Landsat MSS data was classified using iterative self-organizing data clustering using bands 4 and 2. Bands 4 and 2 of MSS are similar in spectral characteristics as bands 4 and 3 of TM images. Fifteen clusters were assigned to one of two categories: forest and cleared. Landscape metrics were then calculated on the classified images.

It was hypothesized that the expected values for *PPU* and *SqP* derived from the regression equations would be similar to the observed values derived from the classified image. The expected value of *PPU* for 79 m according to the regression equation was 0.358. This value is strikingly similar to the observed value of 0.329. The expected value of *SqP* according to the regression equation was 0.989, which is extremely close to the observed value of 0.991. These similarities in expected and observed values demonstrate the predictive capability of the improved metrics with respect to spatial resolution. This predictive capability appears at this time to open the door to the potential for comparison of metrics at different spatial resolutions from various sensors such as SPOT 10 m and 20 m, Landsat TM (30 m), Landsat MSS (79 m), MODIS (50 m, 250 m), and AVHRR (1100 m).

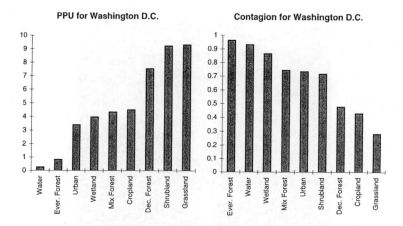

Figure 4.18 Values of *PPU* and *Contagion* for the nine landcover categories of the Washington, D.C. study site. Both *PPU* and *Contagion* show that the grassland category has the highest fragmentation and that water and evergreen forest have the lowest fragmentation. Differences between the two graphs are discussed in the next.

4.2 METRIC CAPABILITY IN QUANTIFYING CHANGES ALONG A SPATIAL GRADIENT IN WASHINGTON, D.C.

This study site provides a contrast from all other study sites. The Washington, D.C. area is a highly developed metropolis unlike urban areas in the Amazon. The study area is also surrounded by an array of natural landcover types such as forest, grasslands, shrub lands, and wetlands. There also is a considerable amount of crop development. The Washington, D.C. area allows for testing of the sensitivity of the metrics between natural and anthropogenic landcover types, as well as for testing among various natural landcover types.

4.2.1 Sensitivity of Metrics to Landscape Pattern Variation

The results of the analysis of *Contagion* and *PPU* with respect to nine landcover categories in the Washington, D.C. area are presented in Figure 4.18. Grasslands and shrub lands appear to be the most fragmented and water and evergreen forest appear to be the least fragmented according to *PPU*. *Contagion* also shows that grasslands are the most fragmented; however, shrub lands show a high *Contagion* which indicates low fragmentation.

In evaluating the graphs shown in Figure 4.18, it is important to view the landcover categories individually to determine which categories appear fragmented or clumped. Nine binary images for each category are presented in Figures 4.19 through Figures 4.27. From observation of the images, it appears that shrub lands are highly fragmented and should show a lower *Contagion* value than was determined. *PPU*, on the other hand, shows high fragmentation for shrub lands, as might be expected.

Figure 4.19   Binary image of the evergreen needle leaf forest category for the Washington, D.C. area study site.

Figure 4.20   Binary image of the deciduous broadleaf forest category for the Washington, D.C. area study site.

PPU shows much greater separability between all nine landcover types than does *Contagion*. The coefficients of variation support this with values of 0.489 for *PPU* and 0.108 for *Contagion*. *PPU* is able to differentiate between natural categories and anthropogenic categories. It can differentiate among natural categories, as well. It also differentiates between the three forest types: evergreen, mixed, and deciduous. *Contagion* is inferior in its capability in separating the nine landcover

Figure 4.21 Binary image of the mixed forest category for the Washington, D.C. area study site.

Figure 4.22 Binary image of the shrub lands category for the Washington, D.C. area study site.

categories. *Contagion* did not differentiate between urban and natural categories such as mixed forest and shrub lands. Observation of the images for mixed forest, urban, and shrub lands indicates that these categories show distinct differences in fragmentation. One would expect a fragmentation or clumping metric to recognize these differences.

Results for the nine landcover categories with respect to *Fractal Dimension* and *SqP* are presented in Figure 4.28. Referring to the graphs, *SqP* shows greater separability for all nine landcover categories. *Fractal Dimension*, on the other hand,

Figure 4.23   Binary image of the grasslands category for the Washington, D.C. area study site.

Figure 4.24   Binary image of the wetlands category for the Washington, D.C. area study site.

shows very little separability between the nine landcover types. An analysis of the coefficients of variation support the fact that *SqP* is capable of distinguishing among all landcover types and performs much better than *Fractal Dimension*. The values are 0.389 for *SqP* and 0.026 for *Fractal Dimension*. Values for *SqP* indicate that grassland has the highest shape complexity, followed by deciduous forest, croplands, shrub lands, mixed forest, urban, wetlands, evergreen forest, and water. In viewing binary images in Figures 4.19 through 4.27, this hierarchical structure in shape complexity seems plausible.

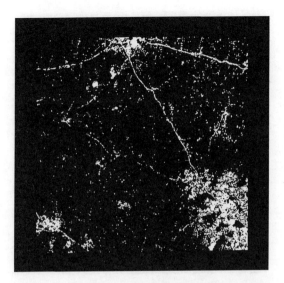

Figure 4.25   Binary image of the urban category for the Washington, D.C. area study site.

Figure 4.26   Binary image of the croplands category for the Washington, D.C. area study site.

4.2.2   Sensitivity of Metrics to Spatial Resolution

The effects of changing spatial resolution on *Contagion* and *PPU* are shown in Figure 4.29. *Contagion* again shows a counterintuitive initial and overall decrease due to the elimination of within-patch pixels. The effects are not as dramatic as those for Rondônia. The reason is that in the case of the Washington, D.C. study area there are nine categories instead of two. *Contagion*, as explained in Chapter 2, not only measures clumping but also diversity. With increasing number of landcover

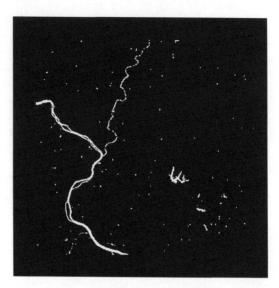

Figure 4.27   Binary image of the water category for the Washington, D.C. area study site.

categories, *Contagion* increases and the effect of eliminating within-patch pixels is reduced. Thus, *Contagion* gives inconsistent and unpredictable responses to changes in spatial resolution.

PPU, once again, shows a log/log relationship between its value and spatial resolution. A log/log regression fit yielded an R^2 value of 0.98 for a linear fit. Notice that *PPU* is not sensitive to changes in the number of landcover categories. Unlike *Contagion*, *PPU* measures only fragmentation and not diversity.

The effects of changing spatial resolution on *Fractal Dimension* and *SqP* are shown in Figure 4.30. *Fractal Dimension* behaves in a counterintuitive manner probably due to problems with regression estimates. Intuitively, *Fractal Dimension* should show a decrease with each aggregation as the landscape becomes more generalized and less complex. For example, Plate 3[*] shows two images of the Washington, D.C. area: one with a pixel size of 30 m the other with a pixel size of 1050 m. *Fractal Dimension* values indicate that the 1050-m image has greater patch shape complexity than the 30-m data. Problems with the spread of data, *y*-intercept estimates, goodness of fit, and a host of other problems with linear regression cause *Fractal Dimension* to behave in this rather unexpected manner. *SqP* shows a negative linear trend with spatial resolution. Regression analysis yielded a near perfect linear fit of 0.998.

4.3 METRIC CAPABILITY IN QUANTIFYING CHANGES ALONG A VERTICAL GRADIENT IN THE SIERRA NEVADA

This portion of the research demonstrates the applicability of the landscape metrics for separating seven landcover classes on a vertical gradient in the Sierra

[*] Plate 3 appears following page 50.

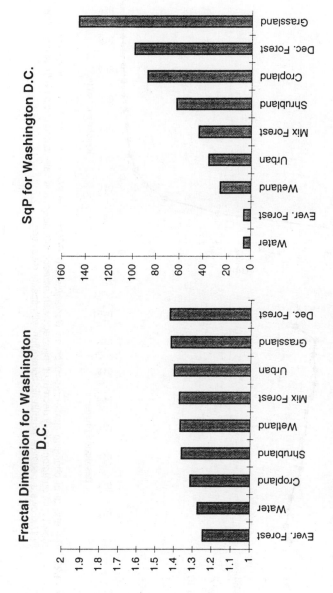

Figure 4.28 Values of *Fractal Dimension* and *SqP* for the nine landcover categories of the Washington, D.C. study site. The graphs show that *SqP* exhibits a much greater separability in landcover types. *SqP* indicates that grassland clearly has the greatest shape complexity and that water and evergreen forest have the lowest shape complexity. *Fractal Dimension* does not exhibit high separability in all nine landcover types.

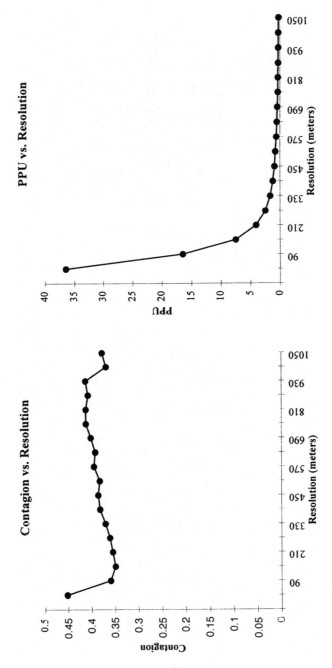

Figure 4.29 The effects of changing spatial resolution on *Contagion* and *PPU* for the Washington, D.C. area study site. The graphs show that *Contagion* initially decreases followed by an increase with peaks and valleys and ending with an overall decrease. *PPU* shows a negative logarithmic correlation with spatial resolution.

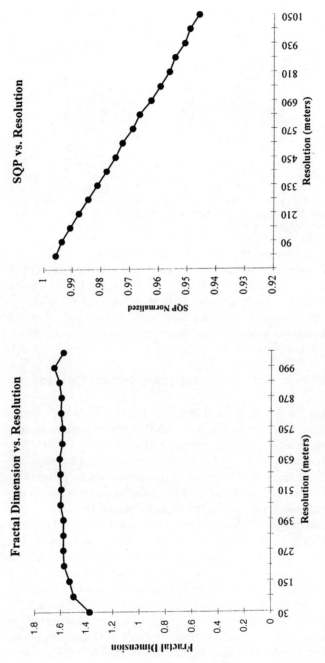

Figure 4.30 The effects of changing spatial resolution on *Fractal Dimension* and *SqP*. *Fractal Dimension* exhibits an overall increase, while *SqP* shows a near linear decrease with spatial resolution.

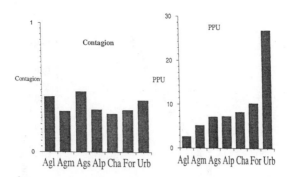

Figure 4.31   The values of *Contagion* and *PPU* for the seven landcover categories of the
Sierra Nevada study site. The graphs show that *PPU* shows greater separability
of all seven landcover categories than does *Contagion*. *PPU* indicates that the
urban category has the highest fragmentation and large agricultural fields the
lowest fragmentation. *Contagion* indicates that small agricultural fields have the
highest fragmentation and chaparral the lowest fragmentation.

Nevada range in California. The transect in this study is located along an extreme
vertical gradient from the summit areas of Sierra Nevada to the bottom of the central
valley between Fresno and Bakersfield. The seven landcover categories are
alpine (Alp); forest (For); chaparral (Cha); large agricultural fields (Agl); medium
agricultural fields (Agm); small agricultural fields (Ags); and urban (Urb). The
sensitivity of the metrics with respect to the seven landcover categories and spatial
resolution was also examined.

4.3.1   Sensitivity of Metrics to Landscape Pattern Variation

Metric values for *Contagion* and *PPU* are presented for all seven landcover
categories in Figure 4.31. The graphs show that *PPU* distinguishes among landcover
types much better than the *Contagion* metric. All landcover types for *PPU* are clearly
differentiated from all other categories by their values except for small agricultural
fields and the alpine category. Urban was distinct from natural categories of forest,
chaparral, and alpine, as well as crops. The distinction between categories for *PPU*
makes theoretical sense and follows the expected model for the area described in
Chapter 3. Urban categories have thousands of smaller fragmented patches and thus
a very high *PPU* value, whereas natural categories are more clumped. The patterns
between the three types of agricultural fields were intuitive as well. Large to medium
to small agricultural categories increase as the landscape changes from highly
clumped fields to smaller, more-fragmented agricultural fields. These trends can be
clearly seen by viewing the binary images in Figures 4.32 through 4.38. Similar
trends are not found using the *Contagion* metric. The greater sensitivity of *PPU* to
changes in landscape pattern is supported by comparison of the coefficients of
variation. *PPU* had a relatively high coefficient of variation of 0.822 compared with
0.120 for *Contagion*.

The metric values for *SqP* and *Fractal Dimension* are presented in Figure 4.39.
Both *SqP* and *Fractal Dimension* are able to distinguish between urban and natural

Figure 4.32   Binary image of the urban category in the Sierra Nevada study site.

Figure 4.33   Binary image of the forest category in the Sierra Nevada study site.

and between urban and agricultural categories. These patterns follow the expected model for the area. Urban networks tend to have more irregular-shaped patches than natural landscapes. Agricultural fields show lower shape complexity since they are usually rectangular or square in shape. *SqP* showed distinct differences in forest, chaparral, and alpine, while *Fractal Dimension* could only distinguish forest from alpine and chaparral. However, *Fractal Dimension* was able to distinguish agricultural fields from the other categories slightly better than could *SqP*. A comparison

Figure 4.34   Binary image of the chaparral category in the Sierra Nevada study site.

Figure 4.35   Binary image of the alpine category in the Sierra Nevada study site.

of the coefficients of variation demonstrates a greater capability of SqP in distinguishing among landcover categories. The coefficient of variation for SqP was 0.376 compared with 0.114 for *Fractal Dimension*.

4.3.2 Sensitivity of Metrics to Spatial Resolution

The effects of varying spatial resolution on *Contagion* and *PPU* for the Sierra Nevada landscape are shown in Figure 4.40. *Contagion* shows an initial decrease

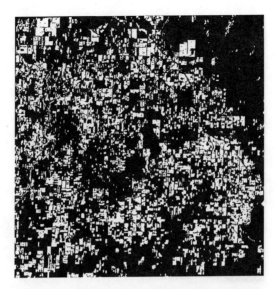

Figure 4.36 Binary image of the small agricultural fields category in the Sierra Nevada study site.

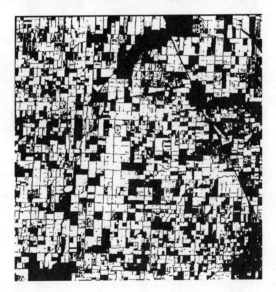

Figure 4.37 Binary image of the medium-sized agricultural fields category in the Sierra Nevada study site.

due to within-patch pixel elimination. *Contagion* then begins to increase slightly with peaks and valleys, after which there is an overall decrease in *Contagion*. The reason for the peaks and valleys is two processes inherent to the *Contagion* equation. The first is the within-patch pixel problem, which decreases *Contagion*. The second is the diversity factor in the *Contagion* equation as discussed in Chapter 2.

The diversity factor tends to increase *Contagion* when there are more landcover categories and to minimize the within-patch pixel problem of *Contagion*. The more

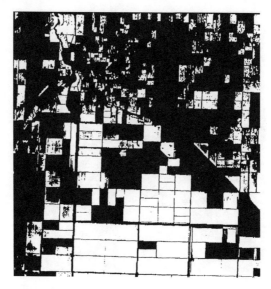

Figure 4.38   Binary image of the large agricultural fields category in the Sierra Nevada study site.

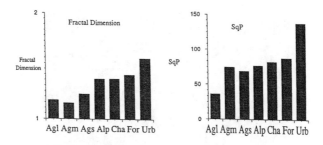

Figure 4.39   The values of *Fractal Dimension* and *SqP* for the seven landcover categories of the Sierra Nevada study site. Both graphs show similar results with the urban category having the highest shape complexity followed by forest, chaparral, and alpine, followed by the agricultural categories.

landcover types on the landscape, the lesser the effect of the within-patch pixel problem. Wickham and Riitters (1995) analyzed a landscape of 23 landcover types and found only minimal changes in *Contagion* with aggregation from 4 to 80 m. The reason for the slight changes in *Contagion* in their study can most likely be attributed to the high number of landcover categories. With these two factors working in the *Contagion* equation, it is unclear what *Contagion* actually is measuring. Obviously, it does not measure clumping alone. An example of aggregating the 30-m image is provided in Plate 4.* *Contagion* indicates that the 1050-m landscape was more fragmented than the 30-m landscape. Observation of the images clearly indicates that the 30-m image is less clumped. Thus, the *Contagion* values do not appear to be performing as they should.

PPU, on the other hand, decreases in the same predictable pattern as in the other study sites. There is a log/log correlation between spatial resolution and *PPU*.

* Plate 4 appears following page 50.

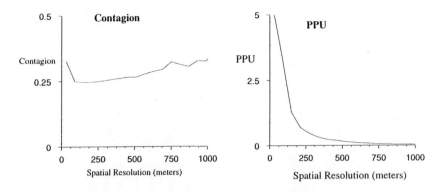

Figure 4.40 The effects of varying spatial resolution on *Contagion* and *PPU* for the Sierra Nevada study site. *Contagion* shows an initial decrease followed by a rather jagged increase with spatial resolution. *PPU* shows a negative logarithmic correlation with spatial resolution.

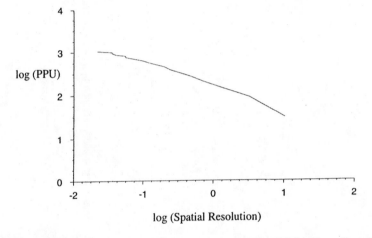

Figure 4.41 Log/log regression plot of *PPU* vs. spatial resolution for the Sierra Nevada study site. The log/log transformations show a near linear plot.

Regression analysis of *PPU* and spatial resolution using a log/log fit produced a high R^2 value of 0.98. The regression fit is shown in Figure 4.41. The line shows a near linear fit after the log/log transformation.

The effects of changing spatial resolution on *Fractal Dimension* and *SqP* are shown in Figure 4.42. *Fractal Dimension* shows an initial increase from 30 to 250 m, which is counterintuitive since aggregating the data should create a simpler, more-generalized landscape. After 250 m, *Fractal Dimension* then begins to decrease as it should. The decrease is, however, very jagged as the graph does not show a smooth decline. The reasons for the patterns of *Fractal Dimension* with spatial resolution are most likely the various errors in the regression fit as previously discussed.

SqP, on the other hand, shows an initial, continual, and much smoother linear decline with each aggregation. Linear regression analysis yielded a 0.99 R^2 value

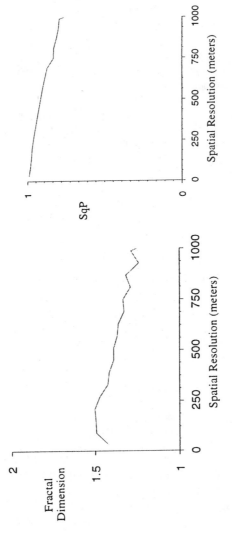

Figure 4.42   The effects of changing spatial resolution on *Fractal Dimension* and *SqP* for the Sierra Nevada study site. *Fractal Dimension* shows a near linear decrease with each change in spatial resolution.

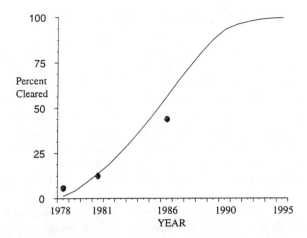

Figure 4.43   Graph showing an increase in percent cleared in the Ouro Prêto study site for model simulations (line) and Landsat data (dots) over time.

for a linear fit. Thus, *SqP* appears to exhibit a much more predictable and logical response to changes in spatial resolution than does *Fractal Dimension*.

4.4 METRIC CAPABILITY IN QUANTIFYING CHANGES ALONG A TEMPORAL GRADIENT IN OURO PRÊTO, BRAZIL

The final study site analysis accomplished in this book was for an area located in the colonization area of Ouro Prêto, in the Amazon state of Rondônia. Analysis of the Ouro Prêto study site shows not only a comparison of the metrics but also an application of these metrics to a simulation model. The metrics were applied to three Landsat images in the study area for three different time periods and to a simulation model called DELTA that simulates forest clearing. In a previous study, Frohn et al. (1996) used *Fractal Dimension* and *Contagion* to assess the capability of the model in simulating spatial patterns of deforestation. Those results are compared with values derived from *PPU* and *SqP* for analyzing landscape pattern. The benefit of using the DELTA model was that it allowed for analysis of the landscape metrics for a longer and more continuous period of time than could be addressed using the Landsat data alone.

Figure 4.43 presents the simulated percent cleared for the 20-year period along with Landsat estimates of percent cleared, which are presented as circles. Clearing estimates for 1978 and 1980 are similar to the model scenario. There was an increase in the rate of deforestation between 1980 and 1986, and the DELTA scenario overpredicts clearing in 1986 by more than 12%. Thus, rates of clearing estimated using remote sensing are somewhat less than the DELTA model projects when using image parameters of Rondônia. Farmer immigration rates could only be estimated for the DELTA simulations, and this could account for some of the differences with the remote sensing estimates.

4.4.1 Sensitivity of Metrics to Landscape Pattern Variation

Estimates of *Contagion* and *PPU* for the DELTA simulations and Landsat images are presented in Figure 4.44. *Contagion* was initially high because the landscape is dominated by large forested patches. *Contagion* decreases as farmers clear more small areas, until *Contagion* takes on a low of approximately 0.4. At this point, landscape patches become more contiguous again as small clearings coalesce into larger clearings and *Contagion* increases. In Rondônia, such increases in the size of cleared areas are generally the result of converting numerous small agricultural areas that are no longer productive into larger pastures (Frohn et al., 1990). *Contagion* increases as clearing progresses, until the entire area is cleared and *Contagion* reaches 1.0.

Contagion associated with the Landsat classifications decreases in a similar manner to the DELTA scenario. However, the DELTA scenario overestimates the amount of *Contagion* in the area relative to Landsat imagery. As is seen in Figure 4.45, the landscape becomes more fragmented than the model predicts. This difference, it appears, is mostly attributed to the way in which simulated clearings are mapped as a simple trend starting from the road and gradually progressing back into the lot. In reality, there are a number of obstacles on a lot that the settler may have to farm around. However, another factor is that image noise in the Landsat scenes may systematically decrease *Contagion* estimates for classified products as misclassified clusters, often one pixel in size, increase the apparent fragmentation of the scene.

PPU shows a similar temporal pattern to that of *Contagion* except that it is opposite to that of *Contagion*. *PPU* was higher when the landscape was more fragmented and lower when patches were more clumped, unlike *Contagion* where values were high for less-fragmented landscapes and lowest for increased fragmentation. The temporal trends in *PPU* were due to the same reasons outlined above. However, *PPU* seems to be more sensitive to changes in landscape pattern than *Contagion*. This statement was supported by a comparison of the coefficients of variation. *Contagion* has a lower coefficient of variation, of 0.288, than the coefficient of variation of *PPU*, which is 0.517. Thus, the effects of stochastic elements and topography show clearer differences between the model and the Landsat estimates using *PPU*.

Fractal Dimension and *SqP* of modeled and Landsat clearings are presented in Figure 4.46. Both metrics indicate the complexity of the landscape, with the lowest values representing simple, square patches. During this study the perimeter/area regression method used to measure *Fractal Dimension* provided a flawed estimate. This problem is observed in the simulation for 1984 in the DELTA case scenario. This flawed estimate for *Fractal Dimension* fell below a value of 1.0, although values are supposed to be constrained between 1.0 and 2.0 (Krummel et al., 1987; O'Neill et al., 1988; De Cola, 1989). Investigation of this discrepancy indicated that the perimeter and area values for this date had very little spread. As a result, the fit of the regression slope for *Fractal Dimension* was not stable and exceeded reasonable limits. *SqP* has no such regression problems because it is based on a direct calculation and not a regression estimate.

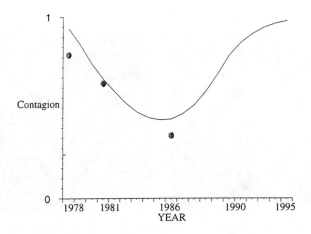

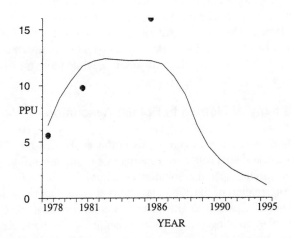

Figure 4.44 The estimates of *Contagion* and *PPU* for the DELTA model simulations (line) and Landsat classifications (dots) in the Ouro Prêto study site. Both graphs show bell-shaped curves over time that mirror each other.

The temporal plot for the DELTA scenario of *Fractal Dimension* shows a bimodal pattern. Estimates of *Fractal Dimension* in Landsat classifications are strikingly similar to the model scenario. However, the temporal dynamics of *Fractal Dimension* for the DELTA simulation are too complex to verify adequately with only three dates of imagery. Values for *SqP* do not show a distinct bimodal pattern. In the DELTA scenario, *SqP* initially increases to year 1981 as the landscape transitions from one homogeneous forest area to a more-complex area with small patches of forest clearing. *SqP* appeared to remain relatively constant until year 1988, when it began to decrease as the landscape became dominated by cleared areas with only small forest patches remaining. Eventually, *SqP* approaches its theoretical minimum of 0

1986 DELTA Model Case   1986 Landsat Classification

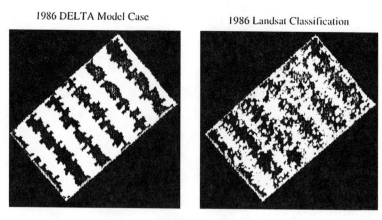

Figure 4.45   Image comparisons of the DELTA model simulation and Landsat classification for 1986. The Landsat classification is both more complex and fragmented than the DELTA image due to farming obstacles, topography, and image noise.

as the landscape becomes completely dominated by cleared areas. The coefficients of variation were very similar for both *Fractal Dimension* (0.182) and *SqP* (0.194). However, the *Fractal Dimension* coefficient of variation includes the flawed estimate of 0.4 for 1984. Nonetheless, these diagnostics are not as important as the temporal trends. The trends for *SqP* make theoretical sense, while those for *Fractal Dimension* are inexplicable.

4.4.2   Sensitivity of Metrics to Spatial Resolution

Aggregations of Landsat classifications in this study area for 1986 (Figure 4.47) show changes in the spatial pattern of clearing as a result of varying spatial resolution. The effects of varying spatial resolution on *Contagion* and *PPU* are presented in Figure 4.48. Aggregation of the 1986 classification creates an immediate and extreme drop in estimates of *Contagion*. This pattern is counterintuitive, as *Contagion* should increase as each resampling creates more generalized and homogeneous clusters of forest and cleared areas. The decrease in *Contagion* supports the fact that this metric is more sensitive to measurement resolution than to actual landscape pattern. This decrease occurs, as previously noted, because the *Contagion* equation uses pixel adjacency proportions without considering the area covered by an individual pixel. The number of within-patch pixels with identically classed neighbors will decrease exponentially, while edge pixels will decrease linearly. Such is not the case with the *PPU* metric.

With *PPU* the 1986 data shows a predictable log vs. log pattern with spatial resolution. As the landscape becomes more generalized due to resampling, *PPU* decreases. The reason is that *PPU* is independent of the number of pixels in the image and only reflects the spatial pattern of the landscape. Linear regression analysis of *PPU* with spatial resolution yielded an R^2 value of 0.98 using a log/log transformation. Thus, by changing predictably with spatial resolution and being more sensitive to landscape pattern, *PPU* gives a better and more predictable quantification of landscape fragmentation than does *Contagion*.

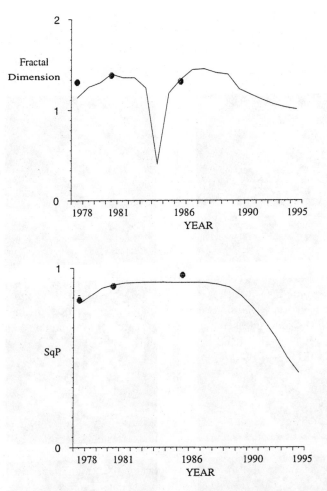

Figure 4.46 The estimates of *Fractal Dimension* and *SqP* for the DELTA model simulations (line) and Landsat classifications (dots) of the Ouro Prêto study site. *Fractal Dimension* exhibits a bimodal pattern with time. *Fractal Dimension* also provides an invalid estimate for 1984 of 0.4. *SqP* initially increases, then remains constant, and then decreases at year 1990.

Varying spatial resolution has a number of noticeable effects on *Fractal Dimension* of the 1986 Landsat scene (Figure 4.49). The effects of varying spatial resolution on *Fractal Dimension* for the 1986 scene contain numerous peaks and valleys. In general, there is an overall increase in *Fractal Dimension* which is not expected since the result of a coarser resampling is typically a generalization or smoothing of features (see Figure 4.47). However, further resamplings result in an unpredictable change in landscape pattern. These changes are due to poor estimates of *Fractal Dimension* due to regression.

The *SqP* metric, on the other hand, shows a reasonable and predictable pattern of change for the 1986 Landsat scene. Overall, there was a decrease in shape complexity as the landscape becomes more generalized. However, the effect of

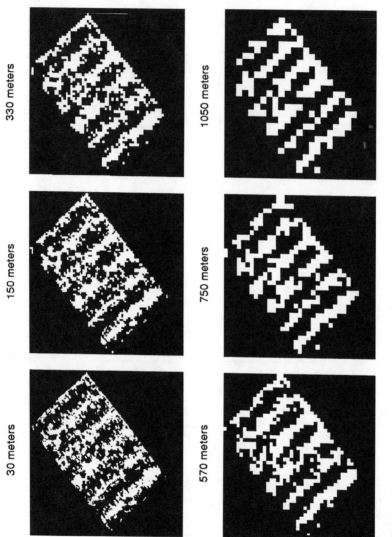

Figure 4.47 Aggregations of the Landsat classification for the 1986 Ouro Prêto study site. Changes in pattern can be seen at meters from 30 to 150 to 330 to 570 to 750 to 1050. Overall, it appears there is a general decrease in both fragmentation and shape complexity with each aggregation.

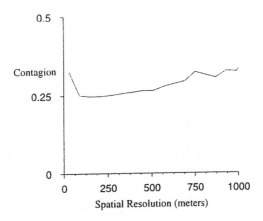

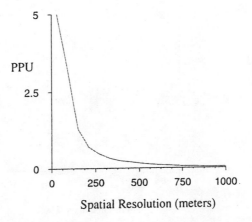

Figure 4.48   The effects of changing spatial resolution on the values of *Contagion* and *PPU* for the Ouro Prêto Landsat classification of 1986. *Contagion* shows an initial decline followed by an overall jagged increase with spatial resolution. *PPU* shows a logarithmic decline with spatial resolution.

resampling creates only small changes in *SqP* because the overall landscape pattern is not greatly affected by the resamplings. Linear regression analysis of *SqP* and spatial resolution yielded an R^2 value of 0.96 for a linear fit. Thus, by having a predictable response to spatial resolution and by being more sensitive to landscape pattern, the *SqP* metric gives a much better and more predictable quantification of landscape complexity than does *Fractal Dimension*.

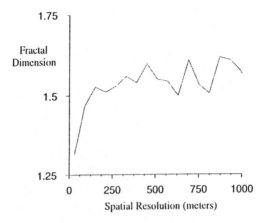

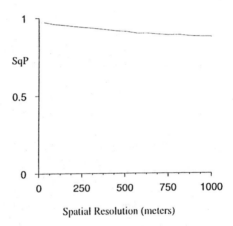

Figure 4.49   The effects of changing spatial resolution on the values of *Fractal Dimension* and *SqP* for the Landsat classification of the Ouro Prêto study site for 1986. *Fractal Dimension* shows no distinct pattern with a sharp and overall increase and jagged peaks and valleys with spatial resolution. *SqP* shows a steady near linear decrease with spatial resolution.

CHAPTER 5

Summary, Conclusions, and Future Work

The goal of this book has been to develop improved landscape ecology metrics that are predictable or independent of characteristic variation in remote sensing data, specifically spatial resolution, and most sensitive to actual changes in landscape pattern. To achieve this goal two objectives were pursued. The first objective was to develop landscape metrics that were sensitive to changes in fragmentation and patch shape complexity along predictable gradients of change. The second objective was to develop landscape metrics that were insensitive to or predictable with changes in spatial resolution. These objectives were met by carrying out a series of tasks. These tasks included a review of landscape ecology metrics currently being used for the monitoring and assessment of landscape change and the understanding of ecosystems; an evaluation of traditional landscape metrics of *Contagion* and *Fractal Dimension* on a conceptual basis using a systematic approach to the design of the metrics; and, finally, the development of improved landscape metrics. The final task was accomplished in order to resolve problems identified with *Contagion* and *Fractal Dimension* as landscape metrics, and to compare *Contagion* and *Fractal Dimension* empirically with improved metrics using "real-world" data for various gradients of change.

The improved metrics developed were the *Patch-Per-Unit* (*PPU*) area metric and the *Square-Pixel* (*SqP*) metric. *PPU* measures the degree of fragmentation of patches on a landscape. *PPU* as demonstrated by this research behaves predictably with characteristic variation of spatial resolution in remote sensing data. *PPU* shows a strong negative logarithmic correlation with spatial resolution. *SqP* measures the shape complexity of patches on a landscape. *SqP* as shown in this research is predictable with characteristic spatial variation of remote sensing data and exhibits a strong negative linear relationship with spatial resolution.

These metrics were tested on data from four study sites based on three predictable gradients of change: a spatial (horizontal) gradient; a vertical gradient; and a temporal gradient. For the spatial gradient two test sites were used. The first site was located in central Rondônia, Brazil where deforestation is shown to be a function of distance from a major urban center. The second site was a large metropolitan area of Washington, D.C. along with adjacent areas of natural vegetation and crops. For the vertical gradient, the study site chosen was a vertical transect in the Sierra Nevada range, California, from alpine areas to Bakersfield, California. The final temporal study site was located in the Ouro Prêto colonization area of the Amazon Basin of Rondônia, where Landsat data and a clearing simulation model of the area were utilized.

For the Rondônia study site both *PPU* and *SqP* performed as predicted, exhibiting the ability to distinguish the amount of deforestation as a function of distance from an urban center. For the Washington, D.C. area study site, the *PPU* and *SqP* metrics were able to distinguish among nine landcover categories, including evergreen needle leaf forest; deciduous broadleaf forest; mixed forest; grasslands; shrub lands; wetlands; croplands; urban; and water. For the Sierra Nevada study site both *PPU* and *SqP* were able to distinguish among seven landcover categories, including urban; chaparral; forest; alpine; large agricultural fields; small agricultural fields; and medium-sized agricultural fields. Finally, for the Ouro Prêto study site, *PPU* and *SqP* exhibited expected patterns for temporal trends.

The *PPU* and *SqP* metrics were also found to be predictable with spatial resolution. The *PPU* metric exhibited a negative log/log correlation with spatial resolution. Regression analysis of *PPU* for the log transformations yielded R^2 values above 0.95 for all four study sites. *SqP* showed a near linear trend for all four study sites. Linear regression analysis of *SqP* also had a high R^2 (>0.96) value for all four study sites indicating a strong linear correlation between *SqP* and spatial resolution. The traditional metrics of *Contagion* and *Fractal Dimension* showed no predictive capability for all four study sites and exhibited counterintuitive results in most of these sites.

These conclusions do not imply throwing out *Contagion* and *Fractal Dimension* entirely. Perhaps they may be used in helping capture landscape variance. Since the two metrics clearly show patterns different from *PPU* and *SqP*, they may possibly be capturing patterns that *PPU* and *SqP* do not. More research into this area is needed to determine what those patterns may be. One general conclusion, however, should be made: the *Contagion* metric does not always measure contagion, contrary to what others have stated (e.g., Wickham et al., 1996), and *Fractal Dimension* does not always measure shape complexity, contrary to what others have stated (e.g., O'Neill et al., 1988; EPA, 1994).

Based on the results described, the goals and objectives of this book were achieved. This book opens a new door for potential research in the areas of remote sensing, geographic information analysis, and landscape ecology. As environmental problems increase at local, regional, and global scales, it is critical that geographers and landscape ecologists come together and focus on the conduct of an array of research related to these fields. Landscape ecology offers quantitative measures of landscape pattern for remote sensing that can be correlated with ecological processes. Remote sensing offers the ability to classify, detect, and monitor environmental change at a wide variety of spatial, spectral, temporal, and radiometric resolutions.

There are many areas in which improved landscape metrics can be used in future analysis of landscapes with remote sensing and GIS. I conclude this book by describing the areas which I am currently pursuing for future analysis. The first is the analysis of landscape metrics with respect to various landcover types. It is quite possible that certain landcover types exhibit similar values with respect to landscape metrics. This concept is what I refer to as a "spatial signature" of a landcover type. It is obvious that it is too early, at this point in time, to determine if this possibility can become a reality. More studies are needed that explore the behavior of landscape metrics with respect to specific landcover types. In this study we found that the *PPU* and *SqP* metrics were capable of distinguishing among seven landcover types in the Sierra Nevada Mountain Range, and among nine landcover categories in the Washington, D.C. area.

There is certainly room for the development of additional improved metrics. For example, metrics that determine the degree of human disturbance on the landscape, the amount of natural and anthropogenic edge, the degree of corridors for animal migration and vegetation dispersal, and the spatial diversity of landcover types are all potentially useful indicators of landscape type or change.

Another area which I am very interested in pursuing is the combination of landscape metrics with spectral information to improve classification of landcover types. For example, landscape metrics could be combined with spectral indexes such as NDVI (Normalized Difference Vegetation Index) for the classification of landcover types that are similar either in spectral or spatial characteristics alone but differ when both are combined. A good example is the distinction between natural forest and disturbed forest in residential areas. Both show the same spectral response but would have much different spatial metric values. Forest in residential areas is fragmented and less complex in shape than natural forest. Thus, by applying the metrics of *SqP* or *PPU* the forest in natural and residential areas could be distinguished and increase classification accuracy.

Another application that improved landscape metrics can be used for is in cross-sensor, cross-study comparisons. Previously, only landscapes that were analyzed at the same spatial resolution were able to be compared. That is why there are very few studies in landscape ecology that are comparative with respect to landscape metrics. By using metrics that are predictable with changes in spatial resolution, results of analyses from various studies can be compared with one another. These comparisons will facilitate the acquisition of an increased amount of information and, I hope, knowledge on the behavior of metrics to a wide variety of landcover types. Improved metrics will also allow for integration of data sources from a wide variety of spatial resolutions and sensors.

Finally, it is my belief that landscape metrics can be utilized in global landcover validation schemes. It is important to determine if landscape pattern is detected, because pattern has many implications on regional and global environmental processes, such as biodiversity, animal migration, vegetation dispersal, predator–prey interactions, plant succession, nutrient cycling, and climate. I maintain that validating the pattern of the landscape may be just as important, if not more important, than validating thematic accuracy. For example, one could have a classification accuracy of 90% for forest between AVHRR and Landsat TM. Yet the forest may be fragmented at the spatial resolution of TM and appear unfragmented at the resolution of AVHRR. The same is true for comparing landscape change. Thus, it is important to make comparisons using landscape pattern metrics. The *PPU* and *SqP* metrics measure the degree of fragmentation and landcover patch shape complexity and can be used for such comparisons. In comparing landscape patterns at different spatial resolutions, it is important that the metrics employed behave predictively with spatial resolution. Otherwise, one would not know if the changes in metric values were due to changes in spatial resolution or actual pattern or both.

These are just a few applications that landscape metrics can potentially provide. I urge landscape ecologists, remote sensing scientists, geographic information scientists, and personnel from federal agencies who are engaged in landscape research to utilize these landscape metrics where they are applicable. More importantly, I urge this array of scientists to learn from the principles and applications that each field provides. Perhaps the most important lesson to be learned from this research is that landscape ecology, remote sensing, and geographic information science each have important aspects that are necessary and can contribute to the development of better ways to model, monitor, and assess ecosystems.

References

Agnon, Y. and Stiassnie, M., 1991, Remote sensing of the roughness of a fractal sea surface, *Journal of Geophysical Research*, 96, 12773–12779.

Allen, J. C. and Barnes, D. F., 1985, The causes of deforestation in developing countries, *Annals of the Association of American Geographers*, 75, 163–184.

Baker, W. L. and Cai Y., 1992, The r. le programs for multiscale analysis of landscape structure using the GRASS geographical information system., *Landscape Ecology*, 7, 291–302.

Becker, B. K., 1987, Estrategica do estado e Povoamento Espontaneo na Expansao da Fronteira Agricola em Rondônia: Interacao e Conflito. Tubingen geographische studien, in *Homen e Natureza na Amazonia Simposio International e Interdisciplinar Blaubeuren 1986*, edited by G. Kohlhepp and A. Schraeder, Adlaf, Brazil, 95, 237–351.

Belward, A. and Loveland, T., 1995, The IGBP-DIS 1 km land cover project, European Commission Technical Report, Ispra, Italy, 8 pp.

Benson, S. J. and Mackenzie, M. D., 1995, Effects of sensor spatial resolution on landscape structure parameters, *Landscape Ecology*, 10, 113–120.

Botkin, D. B., Estes, J. E., McDonald, R. M., and Wilson, M. V., 1984, Studying the Earth's vegetation from space, *BioScience*, 34, 508–514.

Buschbacher, R., Uhl, C., and Serrao, E. A. S., 1988, Abandoned pastures in eastern Amazonia II, nutrient stocks in the soil and vegetation, *Journal of Ecology*, 76, 682–699.

CALVEG, 1991, A Classification of California Vegetation, U.S. Forest Service, Washington, D.C.

Congalton, R. and Macleod, R. D., 1994, Change detection accuracy on the NOAA Chesapeake Bay pilot study, Congalton, R., Ed., *International Symposium on the Spatial Accuracy of Natural Resource Data Bases*, American Society for Photogrammetry and Remote Sensing, Bethesda, MD, pp. 78–87.

Dale, V. H., Houghton, R. A., and Hall, C. A. S., 1991, Estimating the effects of land-use change on global atmospheric CO_2 concentrations, *Canadian Journal of Forest Research*, 21, 87–90.

Dale, V. H., Southworth, F., O'Neill, R. V., Rosen, A., and Frohn, R., 1993a, Simulating spatial patterns of land-use change in Rondônia, Brazil, *Lectures on Mathematics in the Life Sciences*, 23, 29–55.

Dale, V. H., O'Neill, R. V., Pedlowski, M., and Southworth, F., 1993b, Causes and effects of land use change in central Rondônia, Brazil, *Photogrammetric Engineering and Remote Sensing*, 59, 997–1005.

Dale, V. H., O'Neill, R. V., Southworth, F., and Pedlowski, M., 1994, Modeling in the Brazilian Amazonian settlement of Rondônia, *Conservation Biology*, 8, 196–206.

De Cola, L., 1989, Fractal Analysis of a classified Landsat scene, *Photogrammetric Engineering and Remote Sensing*, 55, 601–610.

Departamento de Estradas de Rodagem, Rondônia (DER), 1988, Estado de Rondônia. Porto Velho, Brazil. Map, scale 1:1,000,000.

Dobson, J. E., Bright, E. A., Ferguson, R. L., Field, D. W., Wood, L. L., Haddad, H., Iredale III, H., Klemas, V. V., and Thomas, R. J., 1992, NOAA Coast Watch Change Analysis Program (C-CAP): Guidance for Regional Implementation, Version 1.0, NOAA Coastal Ocean Program, Washington, D.C., 128 pp.

Environmental Protection Agency (EPA), 1994, Landscape Monitoring and Assessment Research Plan, EPA 620/R–94/009, Office of Research and Development, Washington, D.C.

Environmental Protection Agency (EPA), 1996, Mid-Atlantic Landscape Indicators Project Plan, EPA 620/DRAFT, Office of Research and Development, Washington, D.C.

Fearnside, P. M., 1983, Land use trends in the Brazilian Amazon region as factors in accelerating deforestation, *Environmental Conservation*, 19, 141–148.

Fearnside, P. M., 1984, Land clearing behavior in small farmer settlement schemes in the Brazilian Amazon and its relation to human carrying capacity, in *Tropical Rain Forest: The Leeds Symposium*, edited by A. C. Chadwick and S. L. Sutton Leeds Philosophical and Literary Society, Leeds, 255–271.

Fearnside, P. M., 1986, Spatial concentration of deforestation in the Brazilian Amazon, *Ambio*, 15, 74–81.

Fearnside, P. M., 1987a, Deforestation and international economic development projects in Brazilian Amazonia, *Conservation Biology*, 3, 214–221.

Fearnside, P. M., 1987b, Causes of deforestation in the Brazilian Amazon, in *The Geophysiology of Amazonia: Vegetation and Climate Interactions*, edited by R. E. Dickinson, John Wiley & Sons, New York, 37–61.

Fearnside, P. M., 1989, A prescription for slowing deforestation in Amazonia, *Environment*, 31, 17–40.

Forestra, R. F., 1991, *The Limits of Providence: Amazon Conservation in the Age of Development*, University of Florida Press, Gainesville.

Forman, R. T. T., 1995, *Landscape Mosaics*, Cambridge University Press, Cambridge, 632 pp.

Forman, R. T. T. and Godron, M., 1986, *Landscape Ecology*, John Wiley, New York, 619 pp.

Frohn, R. C. 1996, Improved landscape metrics for environmental monitoring and assessment, in *Proceedings ASPRS/ACSM*, April 22–24, Baltimore.

Frohn, R. C. and Estes, J. E. 1996, Validating global landcover classification using spatial-resolution independent metrics, in *Proceedings IGARSS 1996*, Lincoln, Nebraska.

Frohn, R. C., Dale, V. H., and Jimenez, B. D., 1990, Colonization, Road Development, and Deforestation in the Brazilian Amazon Basin of Rondônia, ORNL\TM–11470, Oak Ridge National Laboratory, Oak Ridge, Tennessee.

Frohn, R. C., McGwire, K. C, Dale, V. H., and Estes, J. E., 1996, Using satellite remote sensing analysis to evaluate a socioeconomic and ecological model of deforestation in Rondônia, Brazil, *International Journal of Remote Sensing*, 17(16), 3233–3255.

Gardner, R. H., Milne, B. T., Turner, M. G., and O'Neill, R. V., 1987, Neutral models for the analysis of broad-scale landscape pattern, *Landscape Ecology*, 1, 19–28.

Goodchild, M. F. and Mark, D. M., 1987, The fractal nature of geographic phenomena, *Annals of the Association of American Geographers*, 77, 265–278.

Graham, R. L., Hunsaker, C. T., O'Neill, R. V., and Jackson, B., 1991, Ecological risk assessment at the regional scale, *Ecological Application*, 1, 196–206.

Gustafson, E. J. and Parker, G. R., 1992, Relationships between landcover proportion and indices of landscape spatial pattern, *Landscape Ecology*, 7, 101–110.

Hagget, P., Cliff, A. D., and Frey, A., 1977, *Locational Methods*, Edward Arnold Publishers, London.

Haralick, R., Shanmugam, K., and Dinstein, I., 1973, Textural features for image classification, *I.E.E.E. Transactions on Systems, Man, and Cybernetics*, 3, 610–621.

Hecht, S. B., 1981, Deforestation in the Amazon Basin: magnitude, dynamics, and soil resource effects, *Studies in Third World Societies*, 13, 61–110.

Houghton, R. A., Hobbie, J. E., Melillo, J. M., Moore, B., Peterson, B. J., Shavers, G. R., and Woodwell, G. M., 1983, Changes in the carbon content of terrestrial biota and soils between 1860 and 1980: net release of CO_2 to the atmosphere, *Ecological Monographs*, 53, 235–262.

Instituto National de Colonizacao e Reforma Agraria (INCRA), 1984, Municipio Ouro Prêto do Oeste, Brazil. Map, scale 1:100,000.

Instituto Brasileiro de Geographia e Estatistica (IBGE), 1979a, Porto Velho. Rio de Janeiro, Brazil. Map, scale 1:1,000,000.

Instituto Brasileiro de Geographia e Estatistica (IBGE), 1979b, Guapore. Rio de Janeiro, Brazil. Map, scale 1:1,000,000.

Instituto Brasileiro de Geographia e Estatistica (IBGE), 1982, Estado De Rondônia, Rio de Janeiro, Brazil. Map, scale 1:1,000,000.

Irons, J., Markham, B. L., Nelson, R. F., Toll, D. T., Williams, D. L., Latty, R. S., and Stauffer, M. F., 1985, The effects of spatial resolution on the classification of Thematic Mapper data, *International Journal of Remote Sensing*, 6, 1385–1403.

Iverson, L. R., 1988, Land use changes in Illinois, USA: the influence of landscape attributes on current and historic land use, *Landscape Ecology*, 2, 45–61.

Jordan, C. F., 1987, *Amazonian Rain Forests: Ecosystem Disturbance and Recovery*, Ecological Studies 60, Springer-Verlag, New York.

Justice, C. O., Markham, B. L., Townshend, J. R. G., and Kennard, R. L., 1989, Spatial degradation of satellite data, *International Journal of Remote Sensing*, 10, 1539–1561.

Kienast, F., 1993, Analysis of historic landscape patterns with a geographic information system—a methodological outline, *Landscape Ecology*, 8, 103–118.

Krummel, J. R., Gardner, R. H., Sugihara, G., O'Neill, R. V., and Coleman, P. R., 1987, Landscape patterns in a disturbed environment, *Oikos*, 48, 321–324.

Lam, N. S. N., 1990, Description and measurement of Landsat TM images using fractals, *Photogrammetric Engineering and Remote Sensing*, 56, 187–195.

Lam, N. S. N. and Quattrochi, D. A., 1992, On the issues of scale, resolution, and fractal analysis in the mapping sciences, *Professional Geographer*, 44, 88–98.

Lathrop, R. G. and Peterson, D. L., 1992, Identifying structural self-similarity in mountainous landscapes, *Landscape Ecology*, 6, 233–238.

Leite, L. L. and Furley, P. A., 1985, Land development in the Brazilian Amazon with particular reference to Rondônia and the Ouro Prêto colonization project, in *Change in the Amazon Basin*, Vol. II: *The Frontier after a Decade of Colonization*, edited by J. Hemming, Manchester University Press, Manchester, 119–140.

Lena, P., 1982, Dinamica da estratura agraria e o aproveitamento dos lotes em um projeto de colonizacao de Rondônia. Anais do semonario *Expansio da Frontiera Agropecuria e Meio Ambiente na America Latina: Brasilia*, 10 a 13 de Novembre de 1981. 2 9/1–9/35. Universidade de Brasilia Departamento de Economia, Brasilia.

Li, H. and Reynolds, J. F., 1993, A new contagion index to quantify spatial patterns of landscapes, *Landscape Ecology*, 8, 155–162.

Linnet, L. M., Clarke, S. J., Graham, C., and Langhorne, D. N., 1991, Remote sensing of the sea-bed using fractal techniques, *Electronics & Communication Engineering Journal*, October, 195–203.

Lovejoy, S., 1982, Area–perimeter relation for rain and cloud areas, *Science*, 216, 185–187.

Malingreau, J. P. and Tucker, C. J., 1988, Large-scale deforestation in the southeastern Amazon Basin of Brazil, *Ambio*, 17, 49–55.

Mandelbrot, B. B., 1977, *Fractals, Form, Chance, and Dimension*, Freeman, San Francisco.

McGarigal, K. and Marks, B. J., 1994, Fragstats: Spatial Pattern Analysis Program for Quantifying Landscape Structure, Version 2.0, Oregon State University, Corvallis.

Meltzer, M. I. and Hastings, H. M., 1992, The use of fractals to assess the ecological impact of increased cattle population: case study from the Runde Communal Land, Zimbabwe, *Journal of Applied Ecology*, 29, 635–646.

Millikan, B. H., 1988, The Dialectics of Devastation: Tropical Deforestation, Land Degradation, and Society in Rondônia, Brazil, M.A. thesis, University of California, Berkeley, 186 pp.

Milne, B. T., 1991, Lessons from applying fractal models to landscape patterns, in *Quantitative Methods in Landscape Ecology*, edited by Turner, M. G. and Gardner, R. H., Springer-Verlag, New York, 199–235.

Mladenoff, D. J., White, M. A., and Pastor, J., 1993, Comparing spatial pattern in unaltered old-growth and disturbed forest landscapes, *Ecological Applications*, 3, 294–306.

Moran, E. F., 1981, *Developing the Amazon*, Indiana University Press, Bloomington.

Mueller, C. C., 1980, Recent frontier expansion in Brazil: the case of Rondônia, in *Land, People and Planning in Contemporary Amazonia*, edited by F. Barbira-Scazzochio, Cambridge University Press, Cambridge, 141–145.

Musick, H. B. and Grover, H. D., 1991, Image textural measures as indices of landscape pattern, in *Quantitative Methods in Landscape Ecology*, edited by Turner, M. G. and Gardner, R. H., Springer-Verlag, New York, 77–103.

National Research Council (NRC), 1985, Underexploited tropical plants with promising economic value, National Academy Press, Washington D.C.

Nelson, R. and Holben, B., 1986, Identifying deforestation in Brazil using multiresolution satellite data, *International Journal of Remote Sensing*, 7, 429–448.

Olsen, E. R., Ramsey, R. D, and Winn, D. S., 1993, A modified fractal dimension as a measure of landscape diversity, *Photogrammetric Engineering and Remote Sensing*, 59, 1517–1520.

O'Neill, R. V., Krummel, J. R., Gardner, R. H., Sugihara, G., Jackson, B., DeAngelis, D. L., Milne, B. T., Turner, M. G., Zygmut, B., Christensen, S. W., Dale, V. H., and Graham, R. L., 1988, Indices of landscape pattern, *Landscape Ecology*, 1, 153–162.

O'Neill, R. V., Hunsaker, C. T., Timmins, S. P., and Jackson, B. L., 1996, Scale problems in reporting landscape patterns at the regional scale, *Landscape Ecology*, 11, 169–180.

Pastor, J. and Broschart, M., 1990, The spatial pattern of a northern conifer-hardwood landscape, *Landscape Ecology*, 4, 55–68.

Pedlowski, M. and Dale, V. H., 1992, Land Use Practices in Ouro Prêto do Oeste, Rondônia, Brazil, ORNL Technical Manuscript 12062, Oak Ridge National Laboratory, Oak Ridge, Tennessee.

Peterson, D. L., Spanner, M. A., Running, S. W., and Teuber, K. R., 1987, Relationship of Thematic Mapper simulator data to leaf area index of temperate coniferous forests, *Remote Sensing of Environment*, 22, 323–341.

Post, W. M., Peng, T. H., Emanuel, W., King, A. W., Dale, V. H., and DeAngelis, D. L., 1990, The global carbon cycle, *American Scientist*, 78, 310–326.

Radar of Brazilian Amazonia (RADAMBRASIL), 1978a, Volume 16. Porto Velho. Maps, scale 1:1,000,000.

Radar of Brazilian Amazonia (RADAMBRASIL), 1978b, Volume 19. Guapore. Maps, scale 1:1,000,000.

Rex, K. D. and Malanson, G. P., 1990, The fractal shape of riparian forest patches, *Landscape Ecology*, 4, 249–258.

Riitters, K. H., O'Neill, R. V., Hunsaker, C. T., Wickham, J. D., Yankee, D. H., Timmins, S. P., Jones, K. B., and Jackson, B. L., 1995, A factor analysis of landscape pattern and structure metrics, *Landscape Ecology*, 10, 23–39.

Rock, B. N., Vogelmann, J. E., Williams, D. L., Vogelmann, A. F., and Hoshizaki, T., 1986, Remote detection of forest damage, *BioScience*, 36, 439–445.

Running, S. W., Nemani, R. R., and Hungerford, R. D., 1987, Extrapolation of synoptic meteorological data in mountainous terrain and its use for simulating forest evapotranspiration and photosynthesis, *Canadian Journal of Forest Research*, 17, 472–483.

Setzer, A. W. and Pereira, M. C., 1991, Amazonia biomass burnings in 1987 and an estimate of their tropospheric emissions, *Ambio*, 20, 19–22.

Shukla, J., Nobre, C., and Sellers, P., 1990, Amazon deforestation and climate change, *Science*, 247, 1322–1325.

Skole, D. and Tucker, C., 1993, Tropical deforestation and habitat fragmentation in the Amazon: satellite data from 1978 to 1988, *Science*, 260, 1905–1910.

Skole, D., Chomentowski, W., Salas, W., and Nobre, A., 1994, Physical and human dimensions of deforestation in Amazonia, *Bioscience*, 44, 314–322.

Southworth, F., Dale, V. H., and O'Neill, R. V., 1991, Contrasting patterns of land use in Rondônia, Brazil: simulating the effects on carbon release, *International Social Sciences Journal*, 130, 681–698.

Souza, M. J., 1980, Fighting for land: Indians and posseiros in legal Amazonia, in *Land, People and Planning in Contemporary Amazonia*, edited by F. Barbira-Scazzocchio, Occasional Publication No. 3, Centre for Latin American Studies, Cambridge University Press, Cambridge.

Stone, T. A., Brown, F., and Woodwell, G. W., 1989, Estimates by remote sensing of deforestation in central Rondônia, Brazil, *Forest Ecology Management*, 38, 291–304.

Sugihara, G. and May, R. M., 1990, Applications of fractals in ecology, *Trends in Ecology and Evolution*, 5, 79–86.

Townshend, J. R. G, and Justice, C. O., 1990, The spatial variation of vegetation changes at very coarse scales, *International Journal of Remote Sensing*, 11, 149–157.

Tucker, C. J. and Sellers, P. J., 1986, Satellite remote sensing of primary production, *International Journal of Remote Sensing*, 7, 1395–1416.

Tucker, C. J., Holben, B. N., and Goff, T. E., 1984, Intensive forest clearing in Rondônia, Brazil, as detected by satellite remote sensing, *Remote Sensing of Environment*, 15, 255–261.

Turner, M. G., 1989, Landscape ecology: the effect of pattern on process, *Annual Review of Ecology and Systematics*, 20, 171–197.

Turner, M. G., 1990a, Spatial and temporal analysis of landscape pattern, *Landscape Ecology*, 3, 153–162.

Turner, M. G., 1990b, Landscape changes in nine rural counties of Georgia, *Photogrammetric Engineering and Remote Sensing*, 56, 379–386.

Turner, M. G. and Gardner, R. H., Eds., 1991, *Quantitative Methods in Landscape Ecology*, Springer-Verlag, New York.

Turner, M. G. and Ruscher, C. L., 1988. Changes in landscape patterns in Georgia, USA, *Landscape Ecology*, 1, 241–251.

Turner, M. G., O'Neill, R. V., Gardner, R. H., and Milne, B. T., 1989, Effects of changing spatial scale on the analysis of landscape pattern, *Landscape Ecology*, 3, 153–162.

Ustin, S. L., Adams, J. B., Elvidge, C. D., Rejmanek, M., Rock, B. N., Smith, M. O., Thomas, R. W., and Woodward, R. A., 1986, Thematic Mapper studies of semiarid shrub communities, *BioScience*, 36, 446–452.

Waring, R. H., Aber, J. D., Melillo, J. M., and Moore, B., 1986, Precursors of change in terrestrial ecosystems, *BioScience*, 36, 433–438.

Welch, R. M., Navar, M. S., and Sengupta, S. K., 1989, The effect of spatial resolution upon texture-based cloud field classifications, *Journal of Geophysical Research*, 94, 767–781.

Wickham, J. D. and Riitters, K. H., 1995, Sensitivity of landscape metrics to pixel size, *International Journal of Remote Sensing*, 16, 3585–3594.

Wickham, J. D., Riitters, K. H., O'Neill, R. V., Jones, K. B., and Wade, T. D., 1996, Landscape "Contagion" in raster and vector environments, *International Journal of Remote Sensing*, 10, 891–899.

Wilson, E. O., Ed., 1988, *Biodiversity*, National Academy Press, Washington, D.C.

Woodcock, C. E. and Strahler, A. H., 1987, The factor of scale in remote sensing, *Remote Sensing of Environment*, 21, 311–332.

Woodwell, G. M., Houghton, R. A., Stone, T. A., Nelson, R. F., and Kovalick, W., 1987, Deforestation in the tropics: new measurements in the Amazon Basin using Landsat and NOAA Advanced Very High Resolution Radiometer imagery, *Journal of Geophysical Research*, 92, 2157–2163.

Index

95

L

M

N

O

P